JUNGLE HEROES

AND

OTHER STORIES

by

ERIC B. HARE

Pacific Press® Publishing Association

Nampa, Idaho

Oshawa, Ontario, Canada

Cover design by Eucaris L. Galicia

Copyright © 2005 by the Pacific Press® Publishing Association
Printed in the United States of America
All Rights Reserved

ISBN 0-8163-2063-2

05 06 07 08 09 • 6 5 4 3 2 1

Contents

"Loving Water" and "Crooked Ears"

ALWAYS dressed just in his birthday suit! Pink feet, and hands always in his slobbery little mouth! Always cooing and singing baby love songs! Always dribbling! but he was the loveliest, sweetest baby; and as his mother would catch him up as she climbed back into the house after pounding the rice or feeding the chickens, she would hug him, and cuddle him, and hug him so tight, and then hug him again. And as she always found him slobbering and dribbling, she called him "Loving Water." Isn't that a lovely name for a lovely baby boy?

Twenty times a day his mother would have to leave the house on twenty different errands, and twenty times a day she would come rushing back, and twenty times a day pick up the little fellow, and hug him, and hug him, and cuddle him, and cuddle him, and call him, "Mother's little slobber chops!" "Mother's bundle of loving water!" At least this is what she would have said if she could talk English. But she lived in the jungle, and never saw a white person, so she had to say all these nice things in jungle talk.

Well, Loving Water grew and grew and grew, till he was a big boy ten years old. One day his father came home earlier than usual, and hastily calling all the children around, he excitedly said, "There's a young elephant that has been let loose to feed in the jungle on the side of the hill 'way over there past the little trees and bamboos. Whatever you do, don't go near that elephant, because he's not used to children, and he might harm you."

Oh, how frightened the children were! How wide their eyes popped open at this terrible news! and they all promised that they wouldn't go near him,—all but Loving Water; and while the other children were playing Tiggy Tag, he sneaked down the bamboo ladder and crawled behind the big paddy basket to think.

An elephant! Eating grass! On the side of the hill! 'Way over past the little trees and bamboos! He must! He just must go and see that elephant! He wouldn't get hurt. He'd—he'd climb up a tree! So, peeking out to see that no one was looking, off he ran to the side of the hill where the little trees and bamboos grew.

How his heart went pitter-pat! He could see the little trees and bamboos bending as the elephant moved around. Now that he was up close, he climbed a tree, and soon he was looking at the elephant from a tree about fifteen feet high.

He had such a good view and got such a thrill! So close to a real, live elephant eating grass!

There was his big trunk going swish, swash, as he pulled the grass and poked it into his mouth, and there was his little tail wagging to and fro. "Hum!" Loving Water thought, "father said it didn't like children; it would hurt me. Hum, fathers don't know everything!" Then he began talking to that elephant.

"Heh! Mr. Elephant," he said politely. And the old elephant lifted up his trunk and said, "Groughrough."

Loving Water was delighted. "Oh, he's talking to me," he said to himself. "This is fine! I'll talk to him some more!" So he said: "Heh! Mr. Elephant, what are you eating all that grass for—heh!" And old Mr. Elephant lifted up his trunk and said, a little louder, "Grrrrough-rrrrough!"

It was the greatest fun Loving Water had ever had in all his life. "And father said he'd hurt me;" he said, "huh!" And then he picked a little twig off the tree and said, "Heh, look out, Mr. Elephant, I'm going to throw this little stick at you!" and he threw that little stick and hit Mr. Elephant right on the nose. And old Mr. Elephant lifted up his trunk and said still a little louder, "Grrrrrrrrroughrrrrough-rrrrrrough."

And little Loving Water just jumped with delight. Then he broke off the biggest stick he could, and called out very rudely to old Mr. Elephant, "Heh! look out, old Mr. Elephant, here's a big stick for you to eat!" and he threw that stick with all his might and hit Mr. Elephant right on the nose again.

And this time old Mr. Elephant got angry and, lifting up his big trunk, he bellowed, "Grrrroughrrrroughrrrrough-rrrough. Groughrrrough." And taking three or four strides he walked up to that tree and, putting his head near the bottom of it, pushed with all his might, and down went the tree, Loving Water, and all. Then, with a nasty grunt, the elephant plunged his head with the two shiny white tusks right into the middle of the heap of leaves where the disobedient little boy lay too frightened to move.

He felt the life being crushed out of him. It felt like a big knife cutting him. Surely he was being killed. The elephant thought so too; and not hearing any more talk coming from the tree, he soon went away to another place to eat some more.

By and by Loving Water thought to himself, "I wonder if I am dead. I wonder if this is what it feels like to be dead!" But he could wriggle his fingers and he could wriggle his toes, and he said, "I must still be alive." But there was a lot of blood on the ground, and he felt so weak. Then he crawled out and found that his stomach had been badly torn by the elephant's tusks. Now what would his mother say? And as quickly as he could, he ran home.

The poor mother was so frightened when she heard her little boy calling and when she saw his torn stomach that she said, "Oh, mother's little Loving Water, what ever has happened? Father, come quick! look at our poor little Loving Water."

But when father came, he didn't look so frightened and his wise old head wagged as he said, "I know what makes holes like that in little boys' stomachs! I know! Our little Loving Water has been teasing the elephant on the side of the hill 'way over there past the little trees and bamboos. I know! I know! and, mother, we shall not call him Loving Water any more, but we shall call him Master Crooked Ears ever afterwards." For that is the jungle way of saying Disobedient, and Mr. Crooked Ears is he called to this very day.

He is now a grown man with boys and girls of his own, but he never tires of showing his children his scarred stomach and telling them this story.

Solomon says a good name is rather to be chosen than great riches. Dear boys and girls, we are choosing our names every day, by what we do and by what we say, and how we obey father and mother. Do let us be careful how we choose our names, for when Jesus comes would we want Him to call us Crooked Ears, or Loving Water?

Hte Po, the Headman, and His Seventh-day Adventist Gun

"THARA, I've got a funny kind of old fever. Can't make it out. I've eaten all the medicine in the village, I've been bewitched by the witch, I've been to the priest, but it's no good. Nothing is any good. So I have come down to you to see if you can do me any good," and the headman from La Po Ta village looked intently into my face for some sign of hope.

"Sure, brother," I said, "we have some tiptop fever mixture. It's very bitter; but if you'll take it properly, I think you'll soon be better and," I added, wrapping a little tract around the bottle the while, "say, brother, can you read?"

"Oh yes, a little."

"Well, when your fever gets better, read this little tract."

"Fine," he said, "I will," and away he went with his fever mixture.

Strange enough, but the next year at the very same time of the year Hte Po, the headman, appeared at our dispensary again.

"Well!" I said, "You're here again!"

"Yes," he said, "this same funny kind of old fever has got me again. But that medicine you gave me last year was good stuff, Thara. I must take another bottle!"

"And did you read the little tract?" I asked.

"It was fine," he assured me, and I wrapped another little tract around his second bottle of medicine.

Stranger still, the next year he came again, with the same old funny kind of fever, and took another tract with his bottle of mixture, and the next year for the fourth time in succession, till at last we were getting well acquainted, and we sold him a little book, "Enemies of Health." And by next year I was looking for him as one looks for a regular customer, wondering how he had been getting on. Sure enough, along he came. "Queer," he said, "how I get this funny old fever and have to come to see you every year, isn't it?"

"How did you like the little book?" I asked.

"Fine!" he replied. "Do you know, that little book says it's bad to smoke, so I've thrown my pipe away, and I haven't smoked ever since?"

"Good for you, brother!" I replied, and calling my evangelist, said, "Say, Brother Evangelist, this man is interested; go home with him, and stay a week or two and study with him."

The evangelist came back with the report that in that village was one of the most wonderful openings he had seen for a village school. "Let us do our best," he urged, "to put a teacher in that village, and I'm sure we shall get results." So we put Ohn Bwint out there, and he gathered the children into school and organized a Sabbath school, and at the end of the year he came into our jungle camp meeting at the main station with four bullock carts loaded with people. And Hte Po, the headman, was baptized. The next year the brother was baptized, and the next his eldest daughter, and we confidently hope for more fruit still from that jungle village. And strange to say, Hte Po has no more funny old fever. He declares it was a special kind of fever from the Lord to bring him in contact with the truth; and how we rejoice to acknowledge God's wonderful, mysterious ways!

But my story isn't finished yet. Hte Po was a headman, and was therefore allowed by the government to keep a gun for the protection of the crops and the village against wild animals and robbers. And whenever he went up to church in the village schoolhouse, he chained his gun to a post in his house and locked it with a big padlock to make it secure.

Now it happened that Hte Po had a cousin who was very fond of hunting. And oh, how his heart beat when he saw the headman going to church! He would sneak up into his house and look at that gun and the padlock and wish for a key. And one day—joy of joys—he found a key! and—it did—it fitted the padlock!

Next Sabbath while Hte Po went to church, he sneaked up into the house, unlocked the padlock, and away he went with the gun to the paddy fields where he was almost sure to find a barking deer, nibbling at the young rice. Through the jungle on tiptoe he went. Silently, noiselessly, as the deer he was after, and emerging cautiously on to the paddy field,—oh, what good fortune! A deer not twenty feet away! He raised the gun, aimed carefully, and pulled the trigger—no report! Oh, a dud! He pulled the other trigger. No report! Ouch! Useless weapon! He pulled again, —each trigger twice, but no use, it wouldn't go off. And shamefully he sneaked back and locked up the gun again before his cousin came down from church. And while outwardly he could make no complaint, inwardly he boiled.

A week or two later one Friday evening, as he was coming home from his field, he was startled to hear a tiger killing a pig in a thicket right close to the village. Away he rushed for the headman, but he had gone to chapel for vesper service. Never mind, he'd shoot the gun himself,—

so producing his key, his hands soon held the coveted weapon, as he scurried through the jungle where Mr. Stripes was still enjoying his evening meal. He sneaked quietly up as only jungle men can sneak up, till he was within fifteen feet of the tiger behind a barricade of logs and branches. He could see him through the leaves, and, aiming his gun, he pulled both triggers at once. "Bang!" the jungle echoed and reëchoed with the terrible noise. He looked to see Stripes drop dead as he stood, but there he stood, quietly and determinedly licking his chops—calmly eating—peacefully eating; till by and by, having had an elegant sufficiency, he walked off of his own accord. The hunter looked for blood drops, but not a sign! He looked for signs of the shots having hit the trees near by if he had missed the tiger, but no signs. And he was looking, oblivious to having taken the gun without permission, when a group of villagers headed by Hte Po came upon him.

"Here, where did you get that gun?"

"Oh, I—er—er—I—"

"How did you unlock that gun?"

"Oh, I—er—er—I—" but finding he could not cover his sin, he parried—"Huh, you call that thing a gun? Why, I wasn't fifteen feet away and I gave him both barrels, and he stood there as if it were only a mosquito buzzing around till he had had enough! And I might as well tell you all,— a couple of weeks ago, I pulled each trigger three times at a deer while you were in church, and it wouldn't even go off. I wouldn't call it a gun; I'd call it something else if I were you."

Then Hte Po smiled, came close, and, putting his hand on his cousin's shoulder, said, "Oh no, cousin, it's a gun all right, but it's a Seventh-day Adventist gun, and it won't shoot on Sabbath! When I go to church, it stays at home and rests; and, cousin, I think you'd better rest too, and come to church with me."

Now that was proof positive. It was indeed a Seventh-day Adventist gun. There was no argument against that, so the cousin has since been coming to Sabbath school and church.

The Boy Who Was True Till Death

HE was sick, poor little chap! The joy of his father's heart. The star of his class at school. All day long he lay on his mat and moaned. There was something the matter inside. No, he hadn't been eating green apples,—'cause there aren't any apples in the jungle; but it was something else much worse, and he couldn't eat for days, and his poor little tongue was all coated and furred, and his mouth had that nasty high-fever smell.

His dear mother had been by his side all the time trying to get him to eat, just a little bit, but he could not. "Then just a little chew of betel nut to make your mouth taste better," she coaxed.

His little head shook, but mother pretended not to see that, and went on preparing the dainty morsel,—a little bit of leaf, a little bit of nut, and a little bit of lime, and, to make it something special, she added a little tobacco and some sweet-smelling spices and said, "Now, open your mouth, sunshine, while mother pops in this nice little bite."

But his lips tightened for a moment till he loosened them to whisper, "Mother, I feel that I'm going to die, and I do want Jesus to find me with a clean mouth." He surely knew about Jesus all right,—he had been going to one of our village schools for a year; and a little boy of ten can learn a wonderful lot in a year.

"But, son," she argued, "you don't have to swallow it. Just chew it a little bit, to clean up your mouth, and then spit it out. Come on."

But a strange, pained look came into his face as he replied, "Oh, mother, I promised I wouldn't, I promised I wouldn't; I promised Jesus. I'd be so ashamed if I touched it again. Wouldn't you, mother, if you had promised? Oh, mother, I wish you would promise, and father too."

And just then father happened along. "What's this you want father to promise to do, son?"

"Stop chewing betel nut," replied mother; "and I'm thinking that if we could die as quietly and as happily as this, it would be well for us both to promise." Daddy couldn't talk at all for a little while, but by and by he said, brokenly, "I'll tell you what son—I'll promise—to build a new schoolhouse next year."

"Oh, will you, daddy?" and a smile lit up his pained face. "And will you and mother go to worship every Sabbath?"

"Perhaps, son." Father would have said more, but he couldn't; and, fondly caressing his little boy's head, only after a long time was he able to add, "There, son, try to rest a little and be quiet."

And before long, his face still lit with the smile his father's promise had made, the little fellow fell asleep.

Oh, how I hope to see the little man when Jesus comes to wake up His little jungle heroes!

The Boy Who Went First

"Last time I came through here by myself, I heard an animal right in there!" and my little guide stopped to point into a dense tangle of jungle creepers and saplings.

We were on our way to Lapota outstation, and we had trudged over many a weary mile together,—through bamboo forests, up little stream paths, and the boy's merry chatter had made the time pass quickly. But now we were working our way through an old rice cultivation that was allowed to go to jungle again, where weeds and little bamboos rose like a solid hedge before us. We spoke but little as our hands pushed open the path,—saving our ears for sounds; for such places are dangerous.

As my little friend pointed his unsheathed sword in that direction, I had no difficulty in believing his next statement. "I couldn't tell whether it was a tiger or a wild pig, but I pulled out my sword and ran for my life, and didn't stop till I had passed this tangle and had entered the big trees." I was just thinking that that was just about what I would do if I saw a tiger coming through the thicket to meet us, when he added, "It was wet, too,—early in the morning, and the dew was very heavy, and I was wet through." Then a new thought struck him, and turning round in the small track his eyes sought mine. "Thara," he said, "the morning we come back all this long grass will be wet with dew; what will you do? You will get sopping wet!"

For a moment he was genuinely troubled, but a broad smile told of a solution to the difficulty. "I know," he said, "I'll go first, and as I brush past the wet grass, the dew will all shake on me, and you will be all right,—no, not dry, but not very wet,—not wet as me! That's what I'll do; I'll go first." And away we went again, tramp, tramp, tramp, on our way to Lapota.

We had a lovely time together at the outstation over Sabbath, then early Sunday morning we began the return journey while the dew was still on the tall grass. We were both sopping wet in a very short time, but he marched ahead. He went first, and he seemed delighted when I assured him I wasn't so wet as he was.

I would rather have led the way myself, but I let him go first because he was a jungle hero.

"Daddy, Daddy!"

MYAT PO, my headmaster, sat at dinner in good old jungle style. The little round table about six inches high was just loaded with good things to eat, and at his side on the mat sat his little boy, Solomon. His little two-year-old! Couldn't talk much yet, but could understand a lot; and run? He could run and jump and bounce like an India rubber ball; and oh, how his father loved him, and oh, how little Solomon loved his daddy, and he snuggled up close and ate just as daddy ate. He was daddy's little man. And his daddy had one arm around him, and he loved looking at him and talking to him and telling him to do things. He liked saying, "Solomon, do you love your daddy?" And oh, how his heart beat to see the little fellow's head nod up and down. And after a while he said, "Solomon, my son, won't you get daddy a drink of water?" Up popped the little man,—he understood perfectly, and daddy watched the little chubby legs go clatter patter over to the waterpot.

But it was too high. He couldn't reach the water. His daddy knew it was too high, but he did like talking to his little son and telling him to do things; and how it made his heart rejoice to see his son so anxious to obey him.

Little Solomon stood there watching the waterpot for just a moment, wondering what to do. Then, gathering up all his strength, he reached for the cup, but it also was too high. Up on tiptoes, stomach pressed flat against the post, his little chubby fingers reaching their farthest, he could just touch the bottom of that tin pannikin. Then wriggling his fingers, making the pannikin sound "tinkle, tinkle, tinkle," he called, "Daddy, daddy, daddy, daddy." He did all he could for all he was worth. At the table sat his daddy, the father love aflame in his heart. He listened for just a moment to the sweetest sound on earth while his eyes feasted on the most beautiful thing he had ever seen. Then rising, he went over to his little son, and taking him in his arms, lifted him high till his chubby little fingers could grip the cup and dip the water. Then he placed the little fellow on the floor and let him run back to the table with it. "And even if it was half spilt ere he got there," his father told me afterwards, "it was the sweetest cup of water I've ever tasted in my life."

And that's just the way it is with us and God. He does love us so much. He loves talking to us and telling us to do things. He knows the perfection of His character is too high a standard for us, and we can't reach it by ourselves; but oh, how He longs to see us do all we can for all we are worth and then call, "Father! Father!" Then around us He throws His everlasting arms and He lifts us up,—lifts us up till our imperfections are made perfect in Christ Jesus.

The Little Fifth Standarder

Not long ago we were having our Friday evening social meeting. As I entered the pulpit, the usual Sabbath evening hush fell on the assembly. The first hymn was announced, and at once I noticed two little boys in the front seat talking. I thought it was a little out of place, but gave my attention to the reading of the hymn. This finished, I noticed they were still at it; in fact, even while we were singing those two carried on a very noticeable conversation, stanza after stanza. One covering his mouth would whisper into the other's ear; the other nodding his head would reply. I tried to catch their eyes, but they were far too intent on their conversation. I thought I would have to speak to them, and looked a little more closely to see who they were. Shame! one was a fifth standard boy, small for his age, to be true, but plenty big enough to know better. If a boy hasn't learned not to talk in church by the time he is in the fifth standard, it is time he has, anyway. And the other, the newest boy in the school, and the smallest. A nice example the fifth standard boy was setting him! I could stand it no longer, and, taking advantage of the short pause in between stanzas, I cleared my throat very loudly and looked holes through those boys. But not the slightest notice did they take. All right!—I made up my mind—I'd give them such a lecture they'd never forget. The shame of it! A fifth standard boy talking, and most noticeably, in church, and during social service above all other times! I'd——

The hymn suddenly stopped, and it dawned on me that it was time to pray, but I was too upset to pray. What could I say!—all I could think of was these two boys talking in

1. "Away up in the jungle—"
2. Jungle heroes in the making.
3. Hte Po, the headman.
4. Teacher and class in Hte Po's village.
5. Ma Chey Yin.

6. Myat Po, my headmaster.
7. The boy who went first.
8. Myat Po's little Solomon.
9. Ohn Bwint's contribution to our camp meeting.

church—the idea! So I called on one of the other teachers to pray, and would have kept my eye on them all prayer time no doubt but at the word "pray" they had buried their faces in their hands and turned their backs slightly to each other.

But the minute "Amen" was said, my eyes caught these same two young miscreants, and not a moment too soon. For at once up went the hand covering the fifth standard boy's mouth and into the other's ear was the conversation directed. Then came the reply and the nodding of the head. What could I do! I announced the second hymn; but, instead of reading it, leaned far over the desk while the congregation hunted the page, to see if I couldn't attract their attention. They were whispering so loud I could actually catch what they were—

"O give thanks unto the Lord."

"Ugh! O give—thanks unto—unto the Lord."

"For He is good."

"Ugh! For He is good."

"For His mercy endureth forever."

"For His—His—for His—for His what?"

"For His mercy."

"Oh yes, for His mercy."

"Endureth forever."

"Endureth forever."

"Now again, 'O give thanks unto the Lord.' "—But I didn't wait for any more. The hymn was found, and we sang it with a will. It seemed that the world had changed in that moment of time. Something warm had come from heaven and had filled my heart. Instead of lecturing, I felt like putting my two arms around those boys and hugging them tight. The Lord was good, and how proud I was of the little fifth standarder! He was teaching the new boy a testimony text. And as we sang I saw the nodding grow less, and the hand fall to the side, as the new boy repeated to himself, his mouth easily readable as the congregation sang, "O give thanks unto the Lord; for He is good: for His mercy endureth forever."

The next day was Sabbath, and I preached my sermon from Matthew 7:1: "Judge not that ye be not judged;" and it was one of those sermons that was meant for the "preacher" as well as the "preached to."

The Boy Who Wouldn't Touch His Grandma's Pipe

KA-CHUG, ka-chug, ka-chug. Grandma was downstairs pounding the rice. She had one foot on the ground, and one on the end of the pounder; one hand hanging on the rail to steady herself, and the other hand brandishing a long bamboo to shoo the hungry little chickens away (little jungle chickens are always hungry), and—oh yes, we must not forget, a funny old big bamboo pipe in her mouth.

She had been pounding, ka-chug, ka-chug, ka-chug, all morning, and the even rhythm and the warm sunshine made her feel quite dreamy, when, right into the middle of that dream, with legs ajumping and arms aswinging, came her little grandson. He was home from school on holiday, and his clean shirt, shiny face, and nicely combed hair brought grandma right back to life, and the chugging stopped, the bamboo dropped, and the hungry little chickens jumped right into the pounder for a feed of broken rice (which is just what all proper little jungle chickens do) while grandma greeted the little fellow.

"Well, I declare it's my grandson home from school!" And if his face shone before, it fairly beamed now.

"And how many books has my grandson learned? and how many letters, round like the sun, can my little grandson write? There sure could never be another grandson like *my* grandson."

Now after saying all these nice things at once, grandma should have blushed, but being a jungle grandma, she didn't know how to blush; instead, she just grabbed her stick again, shooed the chickens away, stood on the pounder, and started it ka-chugging, and then gave a big draw to the funny old bamboo pipe, only to find it empty, for it had burned out long ago.

This gave her a new inspiration, and, stopping all her movements as quickly as she had started, she turned again to her little grandson, and holding out the funny old bamboo pipe said, "Here, grandson, go and fill grandma's pipe, that's a boy."

"But, grandma, I don't smoke since I've been learning books at the mission school."

"Don't smoke!" and granny's eyes popped wide open till she could think of something else to say.

"But I didn't say to smoke it, boy; I just said to light it for grandma."

"Yes, granny, but our teacher says not even to touch it, granny," and fearing to disappoint grandma, who had said so many nice things, yet knowing he must be true, he folded his little hands behind his back, and just then a new thought

{ 23 }

struck him. "But I'll tell yer what, gran, I'll do the pounding of the rice for you, and you can light your own pipe, or do anything else you like."

And because I know just how little jungle boys like to smoke funny old bamboo pipes, and because I just happen to know how much little jungle boys hate pounding rice, I call that little man a jungle hero.

A Terrible Punishment

WHAT a grand time they were all having! Little Enoch was only this big. Ser Ser was just big enough to chase around with brother and have some fun; and Moo Say, just home for vacation, was the hero, and the champion, and the doer of all impossible things.

They played at being bullocks, and plowed the road with a stick. They climbed trees, and threw sticks at the green mangoes. They chased chickens, and threw stones into the river. In fact, they did everything that everybody does during vacation.

One afternoon they were in the field romping around, when all of a sudden Enoch held up a commanding finger and said, "Sh-h!" and he said it so hard that Ser Ser and Moo Say stood stock-still, and opened their eyes wide to see what was going to happen next.

"Look over there," said Enoch, pointing with his finger, "do you see that hole in the trunk of the tree?"

"Yes."

"Well, I saw a little bird go in there. Now you stand real still, while I go up and catch it."

And two little figures stood so still you could have heard their hearts beat if you had been real close, while Enoch crawled and sneaked up to the tree. Could the little bird inside hear him coming? How excited he was getting? If only he could stop breathing! He was making such a noise! Nearly there—!

"Hurray!—aye!—quick;" He had covered the hole with a cloth, and the little bird was inside. "Quick! quick!"

But he need never have called, for the others were already racing to his assistance. Moo Say slid her hand in under the cloth and pulled out, not one little bird, but four! Little tiny birds, almost able to fly. The mother bird must have flown away without their seeing her.

"But she will come back to-night, an' we'll come back an' catch the mother bird too. Won't we?"

"Yes, an' we'll make a house for them to live in, won't we?"

"Moo Say, will you teach them to talk?"

"Oh, go on, you silly boy; this kind of little birds can't talk."

"Can't they?"

And all the rest of that afternoon they planned how they were going to look after their birds. There was only one little cloud on their horizon. Mother had said, *"You mustn't go at night, it is too dangerous;"* and though they answered not a word, Moo Say looked at Enoch, and Enoch looked at Moo Say, and pouty lips moved to form the words, "We will go, won't we?" And at evening, when mother was locking up the chickens, they sneaked off—away across the garden, past the school, through the fence, into the field.

"It isn't a bit dangerous, is it?" said Enoch, as they

reached the tree, "mothers think everything is danger—"

"Oh, oh, oh! ouch!" screamed Moo Say.

She had thrust her hand in to get the bird. It was not there, but something else was,—*a big, black snake,*—and it had bitten Moo Say on the finger. Oh, how it hurt! It was just like fire.

"Oh, what shall we do?"

"Now what will mother say?" and squeezing the finger tight, they rushed home as fast as little feet could take them.

Poor mother had enough to worry her without this; but soon she had several strings tied tightly around the arm. Then they tried to think what to do next.

"If Thara were only in the dispensary; but he's gone out preaching with the brass band."

"But the nurse may know something."

They had to do something. The nurse cut it with a knife to make the blood come. Some one else said to try burning it with a red-hot coal from the fire, so they did that too, but still it hurt. Oh, how it hurt! Moo Say was feeling strange all over, and said, "Oh, mother, am I going to die?"

Then some one said to hold it in boiling water for a few seconds, so the finger was held in boiling water, and after that, the poison seemed to come out in the terrible blister that was made.

For days Moo Say was so sick she could neither eat nor sleep, and they hardly expected her to get well; but little by little the pain went away, and she was able to walk around. It was more than a month before Moo Say's finger was entirely well.

And I know two little folks in Burma who won't disobey mother any more for a long, long time.

"The Seventh-day Female"

SHE had taken only three standards in school, poor girl! but it wasn't her fault. Sickness and poverty at home had locked the door of opportunity to her, and she had to hunt work to help keep the family together. When she was born, her mother, from joy and loving hopes for the future, had called her Yea Mye ("Scented Water"), and that this dear girl should have to leave home and go to work was farthest from her dreams then. But was it altogether an accident that after two or three years she found herself in the employ of the Adventist missionary?

"Be careful of those seventh-day people," her friends had warned her. "They are Jews, and they will make you sacrifice and eat the Passover!" But work she had to have; and, to protect herself from the queer doctrines of the Adventists, she bought herself a new Bible.

Imagine her relief and happiness when she found they were not Jews, and did not force her to do anything about religion that she did not want to do. She found, however, that there were so many things that she did want to do, and her new Bible began to be marked as the Sabbath school lessons were learned, and the memory texts in the young people's meetings were noted. How plain it all seemed to be! and how surprised she was to find that the Bible had talked about clean and unclean animals nearly a thousand years before there was a Jew! "I must show the folks at home these things," she said. "How glad they will be to know!" And week by week those memory texts were noted and marked and memorized, and the blessed words began to sink deep into her heart.

Then came a short visit home. The marked Bible in her bag, she suggested evening worship in the home, and prepared to impart some of her new-found treasure. "You're mad!" they said. "You are a Jew. You are a seventh-day female. You are a—" but what could they do? "Call the pastor, he'll straighten her out," suggested one; and accordingly the elder of the little church came. It wouldn't be fair to say that either one was straightened out, but it was no secret that the elder was tied up and left in confusion to find some texts that would settle the matter. By the end of the visit, Yea Mye was nearly starved, as the home folks persisted in cooking nothing but prawns or pork for the curry; so, to defend the Bible that she had been taught to respect, and which she had bought to protect herself from the queer doctrines of the Adventists, she ate rice and salt. On saying good-by, her best friends gathered round, and with shrugged shoulders and tilted noses, made heartless remarks about the seventh-day female. Huh!

It was indeed a problem which Yea Mye could not solve. She was not a Seventh-day Adventist. She was quite sure that they would not get any of their queer stuff over on her; but such hostility from her own folks, as a result of reading a few verses of Scripture, made her unconsciously contrast her home with the pleasant surroundings at the mission compound, and she was glad to be back.

Three years passed. Week by week and Sabbath by Sabbath the texts were marked and learned; and the more hostile her folks became, the more drawn was she to the seventh-day people. How she dreaded becoming an Adventist! But the texts to straighten her out never came, and, anyway, being a true Adventist could not be nearly so bad as being called a seventh-day female when she wasn't; so little by little the texts bore fruit. She would never have consented to a Bible study, and didn't listen to the preaching "pleasantly" when she first came; but those little memory texts in the Sabbath school and in the young people's meeting did the work.

"You may call me a seventh-day female now as long as you like," she announced not long after, during another short visit, "because I have been baptized; and I have some texts here which if you will read and believe, you too will be seventh-day people. Go and call the elder, and I'll call my friends, and we'll have a meeting." But the elder was out, and the friends had pressing engagements. And Scented Water had grasped the meaning of being blessed "when men shall revile you, . . . and shall say all manner of evil against you." And great shall be her reward in heaven.

"Galvanized Iron"

I WAS spending the week-end at Awbawa outstation. Such occasions are much looked for by the village folk, for not only is it a visit from their mission superintendent, but I am also their school inspector and examiner, and it was the time of the half-yearly examinations. No wonder, then, that, as I walked down the center aisle of the little leaf schoolhouse, the boys and girls sat with arms folded, stiff as little images, with hearts going pit-a-pat.

As I arrived at the teacher's table, they stood as one person, and greeted me, "Good morning, Thara," and sat down.

I returned their greeting. "Good morning, boys and girls," and taking the roll book, proceeded to call the roll.

"Bogale"—"Present, sir."

"Dee Dee"—"Present, sir."

"Naw Thu Ter"—"Present, sir."

"Ta Wa"—No answer!

"Ta Wa," I repeated, and turning to the teacher, said, "Chit Mg, what's the matter with Ta Wa?"

"I'm afraid he's coming late, Thara," he replied.

"Late! on examination morning!" and I looked at a whole row of "1's." "Hum! Late every day for a month." Turning the page, I saw another whole row of "1's" and another. Ta Wa had been coming late every day for three months. And I said, "What a pity! a big boy like that late every day! And in the Third Standard too! I shall certainly give Mr. Ta Wa the lecture of his young life the minute examinations are over."

But there was a big day's work before me. I finished calling the roll. All of the other thirty-four were present, and in a moment the questions in arithmetic and geography and Bible were being put on the board. I was busy correcting papers and recording the marks in the record book, and we were just about halfway through the first period, when I heard somebody running outside. Then some one came scrambling up the front bamboo ladder, and, combing his hair with his fingers and still buttoning his coat to complete an evident hasty toilet, took his seat among the boys in the rear.

Turning to the teacher, I said: "Who's that?"

"Ta Wa," he said.

And I said, "What a pity! A fine boy like that, late! late!

late! And what a fine name like that! for Ta Wa means 'White Thing.' I shall certainly give him the lecture of his life! Spoiling all his life like that!"

But I was soon absorbed in the examinations again, and as the day wore on, I became quite tired marking papers and putting down the marks, subject after subject, so that, after dismissing the school at 4:30 in the afternoon, I decided that I wouldn't give Ta Wa his lecture just then. I'd wait till after Sabbath school on the morrow; for then I'd have more time, and I'd be able to put more meaning into it.

The rest of the evening passed in pleasant visiting with the teacher and the evangelist and his family, followed by a wonderful praise service in which every student took part. I enjoyed a refreshing sleep, and Sabbath dawned bright and happy.

What a thrill awaited me in Sabbath school! All the boys and girls had invited their mothers and fathers and uncles and aunties and grandpas and grandmas, till the little leaf schoolhouse was filled. The Sabbath school opened, the superintendent in the chair, the secretary reading the minutes, the whole school joining in song. And then a little boy of ten years was called upon to take the review. I was sitting on the side; and as I saw this little fellow asking the questions and receiving the answers, I swelled noticeably with real pride and pleasure, and we were just about halfway through the review when—I heard somebody running outside. Then some one came scrambling up the bamboo ladder, and, combing his hair with his fingers and still buttoning his coat, Ta Wa took his seat among the boys at the rear. It spoiled the rest of that Sabbath school for me, and I said to myself, "What a pity! Late for school! late for examinations! late for Sabbath school! And a fine boy like that! What a pity! I must certainly give him his lecture as soon as the service is over."

And just as soon as we said our last "Amen," I beckoned to Ta Wa, and said, "Ta Wa! see that bullock cart over there under the jack-fruit tree? Come and sit with me on that old cart. I want to have a little talk with you!"

I did expect his little heart to go pit-a-pat. I did expect his knees would go shakey-shake (as mine used to years ago when my teachers used to call me aside to say a few words to me), but they didn't. His eyes glistened, and, springing down the bamboo ladder, he eagerly led the way to the bullock cart under the old jack-fruit tree. We sat down together, and, clearing my throat, and putting all the severity I could summon into my voice, I started my lecture.

"Ta Wa, my boy," I said, "yesterday—when I was in-specting—the school, I noticed—that you were late! Late every day for three months. Now—"

His face beamed! His mouth was full of words. I had expected he would be sorry, not glad, and I was not ready for his excuses yet, so, shaking my hand in front of him, I motioned him into silence, and proceeded with my lecture.

"Now, Ta Wa, boys who are always late for school, and late for examinations, and late for Sabbath school, will be late for work when they grow up, and late for everything, and finally late for the kingdom," and with a solemn wag of my head I finished my lecture, and tried to make it as impressive as possible. Impossible to restrain his words any longer, his answer just burst forth: "But, Thara, it doesn't matter about my being late! because you see my teacher is good and helps me at nighttime. Because you see, my parents don't want me to go to school at all. My father said I was lazy and didn't want to work. That's why I wanted to learn books, so he said; anyway, I'd have to do my day's work before going to school, anyway."

Now in the plowing season in the jungle the men take a pair of bullocks and a plow, and from daybreak till noon they plow up and down, and round and round in their paddy fields; then the bullocks are released to graze in the field, and the man carries his plow back home, and rests for the next day's work.

"So," said Ta Wa, continuing his speech, "I get up in the morning when the cock crows, at about three o'clock, and, catching my bullocks, I go to the paddy field alone, and it's dark. But I plow and plow up and down, up and down, and by and by the stars fade out of the sky and the sun comes up. Then one by one the men come out of the village, but my work is half done then, and by and by when the sun is halfway up the heavens, my work is all finished. I release my bullocks, and with my plow on my shoulder I rush back home. I only have time to grab my coat, and by washing my legs and hands and face in a pool on the way to school and combing my hair with my fingers as I climb up the ladder, sometimes I'm one class late and sometimes I'm only half a class late; but that doesn't matter, because my teacher is so good,—he helps me at night, and, Thara, I'm sure that I'll be able to pass my examination at the end of the year with the other boys."

Then he stopped, and waited for me to say some more, but away down here where the words come from, something had happened. My lecture had all gone wrong. I didn't have any more words left, only a big lump which I was trying hard to swallow. My eyes filled as I wondered whether with all my opportunities I could measure up to the same degree of faithfulness before God as this jungle lad did, getting up at three o'clock every morning, and doing a day's work before going to school. But by and by I added:

"Ta Wa, I'm going to change your name."

"What are you going to call me, Thara?"

"Well, I'm going to put an 'H' before that 'Ta' and call you 'Hta Wa' because Hta Wa means 'Galvanized Iron,' and I reckon that a boy who can get up at three o'clock every day to get his work done before going to school is surely made of galvanized iron. It's good stuff, laddie. Stick at it, and may God make you into a worthy worker for Him."

Ma Chey Yin to the Rescue

OH! such a river, beautiful, clear water, long-reaching sand banks,—so can you wonder that everybody in our school, which is right on the bank of this river, can swim? Did I say swim? Aw, that's not half what they can do. They can dive, and swim under the water, and make funny air balloons with their *longyis* and go floating around, and back pedal and turn somersaults, and imitate motor boats; and even this isn't half yet. They can ride bamboos, and sail boats, and paddle canoes, and dig holes, and bury people up to their necks in sand, and then watch the earth quake while they are getting out. Dear old river! Everybody loves the dear old river!

No, there aren't any crocodiles in our river; and there's nothing to be frightened of, only—but—well, of course in the rainy season it is very dangerous! The water gets very muddy. It rises thirty feet. It breaks away the river banks here and there. It makes whirlpools, and just as if it were angry, it grows and roars, and tears up trees and bushes as it rushes down through the hills to the plains.

Now it happened one day when the river was high that five or six little girls decided to go for a swim.

"Be careful," called Bu Yin as she saw them going down the track.

"We won't go far out."

"But the current is swift and the whirlpools—"

"Booh! We can swim."

"Nobody can swim in whirlpools, you foolish children."

"But we aren't going into the whirlpools," and with that they disappeared over the bank and were soon having great fun.

"Hum! Whirlpools! Pooh! why, even I—and I'm the littlest in the whole school—am not afraid of whirlpools. Look at me!" called little Ma Sein, and she jumped and dived and swam and motor-boated.

But just then the edge of a whirlpool drew her a little farther than she intended to go. When she felt herself going out, she became scared, but a moment's struggle told her it was no good to try to swim, she must save all her strength to keep afloat, and with whitened face and powerless arms she drifted off down the river in the current.

"Help! help!" the girls squealed and cried.

"Help! Help!"

But the angry river made so much noise that no one could hear the little girls calling. They followed along the bank, and yelled and squealed.

"Ma Sein is drowning!"

"Help! Help!"

But nobody could hear, the cruel whirlpool had her now, and as a cat plays with a mouse before it finally opens its mouth to swallow it, it swung her away out, then in near to shore, around and around, out and in.

Poor Ma Sein struggled as she could to keep afloat. A little longer and her strength would be gone. A little longer and the whirlpool would have sucked her into its mouth.

"Girls, we've got to do something!" Ma Chey Yin had suddenly come to life. No more white face, no more squeal, no more shaking knees, but jaw set and eyes fixed, she waited till the whirlpool brought Ma Sein near to shore again in its terrible merry-go-round game. Then a plunge, a few swift strokes, and silence, except for the angry snarl of the river.

"She's got her by the hair."

"Good! Ma Chey Yin!"

"Pull! Pull!"

"You getting her! You getting her!"

"Do it again!"

"Hurray! She's out of the whirlpool."

Two more now plunged in, and the rest was easy. And soon six very frightened, sorry-looking little girls sat huddled together with their arms around one another.

"Oh! don't tell Bu Yin," whispered Ma Sein.

"We'll never laugh at whirlpools again!"

"Oh no! don't let's tell anybody."

But you can't help talking about heroes. They had to tell how brave Ma Chey Yin was; and now everybody knows, so I'm telling you.

1. The schoolhouse a little hero's father built.
2. View from Kamamaung Mission Station.
3. "Galvanized Iron."
4. My Lenny.
5. Some pupils at the Awbawa school.
6. "The seventh-day female" lived in our family for many years.
7. Thara Hlo Hpo.
8. The boy who was true till death.
9. Where Thara Hlo Hpo taught just one year.

The Boy Who Wouldn't

You know how it feels when school's out, don't you? I mean at the end of the year, when we are going to have holidays. When we have been in school all year long, and studying hard, and at last, the last night comes, and we have a musical evening, and the grade cards are given out; it feels great, doesn't it! And we shake hands with our schoolmates and laugh and cry—and—well, anyway, you know how it feels. That's just the way the little jungle boy that I'm going to tell you about felt.

He couldn't sleep all night, he was so happy, thinking of the grand times he was going to have at home with his little brothers and sisters; thinking of the fun he would have in the little creek that ran near the village, where the water wasn't very deep, and you could see the sand and the pebbles on the bottom; and thinking of the coconut trees he would climb, and the rides he was going to give baby sister on his back. He never knew a night to be so long.

No sooner had the cock crowed about three o'clock in the morning than the boys began getting up. Some were going down the river by boat, some were going by bullock cart, and the ones who lived near were going on foot; but they could not go till daylight. Thara was up getting the companies started, and shaking hands; and every time a group started off, Thara called out, "Don't forget the temptations," and all the boys called back, "No! we won't chew the dirty red stuff," and then they started off singing.

My, I tell you it feels great; I reckon it's worth studying hard all the year just to get the feeling of going home. And you'd like to be going and staying and riding and walking all at the same time; but this little boy was walking, so he was among the last to pick up his little bundle and start off.

And weren't they glad to see him home, too! though they didn't say much (jungle folk never do). They had everything all ready for him, and a regular feast prepared. The rice was piping hot, and so nice and flaky—mother had taken special pains because her little man was coming home from school. And curry! my, but it smelled good, and he had just discovered that he was awfully hungry; and sitting on the floor he reached over and helped himself to plenty of curry; but—it—was pork curry!

"Mum, is this pork?" he groaned; and his mother, all smiles, said, "Yes, we bought it specially 'cause you were coming home."

"But, mum, we are taught at school that pork isn't clean."

"Isn't what?"

"Isn't clean, mum!" Then he told his mother all about it, and how God didn't like us to eat unclean things; and then the battle started. Would he? or wouldn't he? It wouldn't matter just once. Would he? But Thara had said, "Don't forget the temptations." Was pork a temptation like betel nut? He couldn't! How could he? My, but he was hungry! If he only,—but—"No, mum, I can't; never mind, I'll eat rice and salt this time." And shoving his plate over to his little brother, he said, "Here you are, brother! It's all right for you, 'cause you don't know about it; you don't go to school yet. But I go to school, and I know, and I can't. I'll eat rice and salt."

And just 'cause I know what plain rice and salt tastes like when I'm awfully hungry and just home from school,—I call that little man a jungle hero.

Three Boys Who Did a Noble Deed

SCHOOL was out. The hot sun, shining down with all his might, making up for the months when he would be hidden by the black rain clouds in the wet season, made study almost impossible. But it was just the right kind of weather for jungle preaching, and five band boys from Kamamaung had joined the evangelist and teacher at Awbawa, and mapped out a tour of the district.

We had had a school in that village only one year, but the boys were enthusiastic, and all solemnly promised to help the evangelist's wife look after Sabbath meetings while the others were away. Just before they set out, however, the dear old man who had taught school during the year was called home to see one of his big sons who was sick with the fever, and the preaching party had to set out without him over the hills and far away.

You can imagine that old Thara Hlo Po, for that was his name, was very sorry not to be able to accompany the preaching band; but, being anxious for his son, he hurried to the heathen village fifteen miles away, where he was living. Finding the lad in a serious condition, the father walked twenty miles to a hospital for some medicine and twenty miles back without resting except for food. The road was good, but the return journey was made in the heat of the day; and though he arrived with the medicine in time to save his son's life, he himself was smitten with sunstroke and died a few days later.

At once a messenger was sent to Awbawa for the evangelist, for they could not consent to let the village folk give him a heathen burial; but who could tell where the evangelist and the band boys had gone by this time? In vain they questioned among the children and the village elders, but after so many days they might be almost anywhere. No one could think of a way out, till one little man just twelve years old said to a group of his schoolmates who had gathered round to discuss the situation, "We can never let our Thara be buried in a heathen way. Don't you suppose some of us could go and read a chapter and sing and pray? I tell you, I will go if one or two of you will come with me." In a twinkle two more little men, one eleven and one nine, had volunteered, and, obtaining hasty permission from their parents, set off on the fifteen-mile walk to the other village.

On arriving, they went up into the house and sang— sang the gospel songs the dear old teacher had taught them through the year. The village folk crowded round to see the sight,—and such a sight it was! They sang till all their songs were finished and their little hearts so full that it hurt to sing any more, then one read a scripture. He didn't know which chapter in Job the ministers read at the funeral services—he had never seen a Christian funeral, but he read a part of the Sabbath school lesson he had been studying during the week. The next little laddie led in prayer; and, leading the way to the grave, they laid away the dear old man to await the resurrection morning.

Three weeks after, the preaching band came back, and the little fellows had almost forgotten their deed of love; but I know that angels wrote this story in the books that are kept in heaven, in which are recorded all the loving deeds done in Jesus' name by brave little jungle heroes.

The Little Girl Who Saved the House From Catching Fire

THE evening was quiet, and lazy, and hot. Half a moon half tempted one to sit outside, but there was no breeze. So worship finished, the few who stayed behind at school during vacation scattered around to play or talk or eat.

I was at supper, all bathed and freshly clad, and taking life as easily as I could, not caring to produce more perspiration than was absolutely necessary (I had perspired enough that day), when the rushing of feet up the back stairs, the breathless words, "Quick! Thara! Fire! Girls' House! Fire! Lamp! Fire!" with the now-increasing cry outside of "Fire! Fire! Fire!" pressed my electric button. Springing up, not staying to ask any questions, but seizing the Pyrene pump, I bounded down the steps.

It could have taken only three minutes to run the distance, possibly only two, but my mind pictured our new Girls' Hall in ashes. The newest building on the mission, used only three months, charred and blackened and ruined. You can imagine then my surprise to arrive on the scene to find all quiet and in darkness. No fire! nor even a light, except the half moon smiling down on us. Yes, quiet, but only till I got there! That quietness born of white faces and shaking knees. Then twenty voices burst from twenty throats all together, one after the other:

"Oh, Thara! It was terrible! I didn't know what to do. I grabbed my two children, and I don't know how I got down the stairs," gasped the wife of the teacher in charge.

"It was the gasoline lamp," panted another. "Don't know what the matter with it was, but we thought we ought to

turn it out and take it over to San Nyok to fix. So some one
turned it; but, instead of turning it off, she opened it more
and more and more and more and turned and turned and
turned till the gasoline leaked out, and with a sudden
"woof" the whole thing was in flames. Then everybody
screamed, and we ran for you, and we don't know what
happened after that. Say, girls, what did happen after that?"

"Oh, I ran for my life," said one.

"I too," said another.

"I didn't even stop to get my box."

"Yes, but who brought the lamp out? Why didn't the
house catch on fire?"

"We thought it was on fire!"

"It was Kyu Sein who brought the lamp out," called a
voice from somewhere, and all eyes turned to little Kyu
Sein. Yes, little, for she's almost the littlest girl we have in
school, and now, self-conscious, with all eyes so suddenly
turned on her, she stood half on one leg and half on the
other with one hand in her mouth. You know how you
do when you're nervous.

"Come, tell us all about it!" we all entreated. So she
started.

"Well, when everybody ran, I knew something would
have to be done with the lamp, and I knew if we waited till
you came, maybe the wood would be on fire, so I picked
up the window bar, and managed to poke it through the
handle; then little by little I got the blazing thing outside,
where it soon went out."

"But weren't you terribly scared?"

"Oh yes, but some one had to do it, an'—"

And that's why we all gave *three cheers for Kyu Sein!*

The Little Boy Who Didn't Eat All His Dinner

I DON'T like dogs. Don't know how it is, but I never did as long back as I can remember. Sometimes I think it must have been because when I was a little chap and used to give out handbills for my daddy who preached in a tent, the dogs used to chase me, and scare the life out of me, and say all kinds of nasty things that I didn't like; but all I know is that when I grew up I didn't like dogs, and never had one around the house, till one day my little boy brought home a little black pup. And he said, "Oh, daddy, look at my nice little black puppy!"

But I said, "No, son, it isn't a nice little black puppy; it's a nasty old black dog."

But I tried to be patient, because you know usually little boys have lots of fun with little black dogs; and I didn't want my son to be scared of dogs just because I was, so I finally allowed him to keep it down under the stairs in a box.

One day, a long time after it came to live with us, I came home from a jungle trip to find quite a deal of excitement. Yes, and quite a deal of yip, yip, yipping. For there in a box were three more brand-new little black doggies. Wasn't my little son happy! But I wasn't! 'Cause I don't like dogs. Don't know how it is. Those little pups yipped and yipped. They yipped at night when I wanted to sleep. They yipped at dinner time, when I wanted to eat. They yipped in between times when I wanted to work in my office. So one day I said to my little boy, "Well, son, now the pups are getting bigger, you must find homes for them, and give them away! One doggie around the house is enough."

"But daddy, they's nice little dogs!"

"They are noisy little yip-yaps, son," said I.

"But, daddy! daddy!—"

"Now, son, you've heard what I've said. Now go to it. I'll give you a week to find homes for those little pups." And because he knew that once his father had spoken there was nothing to do but obey, he said no more.

A few days after that, mother and Eileen went to town, leaving Lenny and me at home by ourselves. He didn't mind staying home. He loves being with his daddy, and all day his little legs trotted around after me. To the school, to the saw pit, to the dispensary, to the office. Then lunch time came, and we sat down to have a feast together—some good bread and butter and stewed fruit and a big glass of milk each. Oh, that's what we like! and we were hungry too. But as we ate, I noticed little Lenny wasn't drinking his milk!

"Hullo, son, your milk not nice?"

"Er—oh, yes! but—I—"

"Not getting sick, are you?"

"Oh no, course not. Only—er—"

"Well, then, what's the matter?"

"Oh, nothing—er—um—only—"

"Only what?"

"—Er—perhaps I'll have it after a while."

"Oh, well, all right, if you don't want it now, you may leave it for supper." But something in his actions made me a little bit suspicious. We finished lunch, and I went into my room, leaving Lenny still at the table.

Little tiptoe sounds, however, soon made me curious, and I peeped through a crack in the door. There was my little boy, his two hands around his glass of milk, tiptoeing out of the house.

I followed, tiptoeing at a distance. What could be the meaning of this strange behavior? Down the stairs he went. Then I wasn't left very long in doubt.

"Yip, yip, yap, yap, yip, yap."

"All right, you dear little doggies, here I come! And I'm bringing you some nice milk to drink."

"Yip, yip, yip, yip, yap, yap."

"Daddy says you got to go away from me after this week, and I don't know how I'll live without you, an' I don't know if you'll get any milk to drink in your new homes, but, anyway, I'll see that you get plenty of milk while you live with me."

"Yip, yip, yip—"

"Yes, you poor little puppies, you won't have any home after this week, and no nice milk to drink, an'—"

I sneaked away as fast as I could. I couldn't intrude on such a painful parting. And, trying hard to say it in a casual way during the afternoon, I said, "Well, son, perhaps the puppies are a bit too small to give away yet. How'd you like to keep them till they grow up?"

"Oh, daddy! goody!" and he was off, dancing down the path.

And that evening when I went in to kiss him good night, a smile still played on his dreaming face. And beneath the bed the four little black doggies slept, smiling too, close to his heart. Strange, I don't like dogs. Don't know how it is. But we haven't got any dogs for sale here in our house.

The Happiest Mother in All the Land

IT had been a hot, tedious day. The river steamer, its decks crowded with a cargo representing the needs of a jungle people all the way from cart wheels to bags of rice and evil-smelling pots of "fish paste," had left just as the tide had turned against it, and had chugged courageously enough, but slowly, up the river.

The passengers, bizarre and loquacious, had chatted and argued, smoked and chewed, slept and eaten, till now they looked a weary, grimy lot, sitting among the shells and peels and wrappings. Tired? Yes! and so was the captain, and irritable. And as the ship was run into the river bank here and there, his voice, sharp and accented, lent impetus to those scrambling on and off by means of the gangplank, long and narrow, which bridged the gulf between the steamer and the land—and sometimes didn't.

Earlier in the day, the landing of the passengers had been the chief source of entertainment, and loud indeed was the laughter and prolonged indeed were the cheers that accompanied a misstep with its consequential ducking, or a long, shallow landing that necessitated wading and clothes wetting. But as the day wore on, the amusement gave way to impatience, laughter to sighs, and cheers to murmurings. Can you wonder, then, arriving at Wotkyi three hours late, with the sun just setting, and ten more miles to go, that the captain tugged at the whistle angrily and urged those to embark with staccato curses, that the clerk's assistant clanged his bell impetuously, calling out for all to get their tickets, and that for want of anything else to do, all the rest of us glared over the side of the boat at the crowd who were scrambling on with their bags and baskets?

One by one they came aboard, pushing, scrambling, jostling, about thirty of them, till at last there remained but one lone passenger, seemingly not the least excited about getting on board. Every passenger opened his mouth to urge the slow one to action, the assistant grabbed his bell and climbed on to some bags of rice where he could be better heard. The captain, filling his mouth with curses, reached for the whistle rope,—but the mouths closed silently, the bell rested noiselessly on the rice bags, the curses were swallowed, and the captain's hand dropped lifelessly from the whistle rope, because we all had realized the same thing at the same time,—the lone remaining passenger was a little feeble old lady, and she was blind.

It was one of those helpless moments when every one knew that something ought to be done, but everybody waited for some one else to do it. She was somebody's mother! Some began to pray. Others tugged at their handkerchiefs, while lumps of sympathy swelled in their throats. But the little old lady stood there, quiet and unmoved.

Why didn't some one help her? Why did she stand so still? Why didn't she—? but just at that moment a strong young man, having deposited his bags and baskets on board, bounded down the gangplank, and going close to the little lone figure, whispered loudly in her ear, "Put your arms around my neck, and don't be frightened, mother." Then, bending his noble back, he lifted the little frail form in his arms and carried her safely aboard.

The captain cried, "Bravo!" The crowd cheered, the bell resumed its clanging. The engines started, and we were on our way once more. I bounded downstairs to greet the hero of the day, just in time to see the little old lady brush two big tears from those sightless eyes. "Don't be sorry, auntie," I comforted.

"Sorry, Thara?" she queried. "Sorry! why I'm not sorry, Thara. I'm the proudest, happiest mother in all the land."

―――

Lenny's Motor Car

IT was 4:30 A. M. when with a little grunt four-year-old Lenny wriggled over the little wall of his bed, and rolled over into daddy's and mamma's bed; right over the top of mummy, puffing and blowing till he settled down nice and snug right in the middle, and stretched out his chubby little arms one to go around daddy's neck and one to go around mummy's neck. Then in his own way of making love he took up an argument with himself under his breath. "This is my mummy, this is my daddy. It *is* my mummy, it *is* my daddy. It isn't your mummy," and he hugged so tight; how could anyone sleep or sham sleep with a little cuddle bug like that in bed with him? So daddy just opened one eye. In a twink Lenny saw it, pulled his arm from under mummy's head, and feeling all over daddy's face, succeeded in pulling open the other eye. Then pulling daddy's face up, oh, so close, he said, "Daddy, you is my daddy, isn't you?"

"Of course I am, son," and daddy did some hugging too while Lenny sang over to himself, "He is my daddy, he is my daddy, my great big daddy." Then becoming very confidential he asked, "Daddy, some day you will make me a motor car?"

"A what, son?"

"A motor car, daddy, with a too-too like a train. Will you, daddy? Eh? Some day you will make for me a motor car an' a seat in it?"

"What do you want a motor car for, son?"

"To pull, daddy, and to ride in, and to give the pussy cat a ride in. A great big motor car, an' paint it green. Daddy, you will make for me?"

"Oh, I suppose so, son," assented poor sleepy daddy. "But where's daddy to get the wheels and the boards and the—"

But Lenny didn't care about that side of it one bit. That didn't concern him. Daddy said he was going to make him a motor car, and that was enough. How glad he was! He must tell mother; so, freeing himself with all speed, he applied himself to mummy. He opened her eyes, squeezed her nose, and made poor tired mother turn over and groan. But he turned over too, and shook and mauled and called in all the different voices at his command, "Mummy! *mummy!* MUMMY!" till at last, not being able to hold out any longer, mummy turned back, and was just beginning to show the first signs of coming to, when he broke the joyful news. "My daddy is going to make me a big, big motor car! He is, mummy. He is. He said he is. And I'll give See See a ride and Barnabas a ride and the pussy cat a ride. Mummy, do you want a ride in my motor car, mummy?"

Just then clang, clang! went the bell, and father had to bound into his clothes and be off to worship. On the way back he met his young son on the road. "I's going to tell See See, daddy. I's going to give See See a ride in my motor car. Daddy, you going to make for me, with a too too an' a seat? Oh, you are going to make. You tell me," and off he went full steam ahead to break the news to See See.

After worship came work period. There was the work on the farm to keep an eye on, and the boys building the school to help. Father was talking to Peter, shaping and planning the work, when Lenny, espying him all the way from See See's house, gave chase, and in a minute was dangling around daddy's legs, calling, "Daddy! daddy!" Daddy didn't seem to have ears. He kept on talking and talking and talking to Peter, so Lenny kept on calling louder and louder, "Daddy! *daddy!* DADDY!" till neither daddy nor Peter could hear themselves think.

"What, son? What, son? What? What's all the noise about? Can't you see daddy is busy!"

"Daddy, when you going to make my motor car?"

And daddy,—just the ordinary "being evil" variety— rather impatiently replied, "Oh, son, boil your old motor car! Can't you see daddy has got to build the school and teach? You'll have to wait a long time for the motor car, son."

"A day, daddy?"

"Huh! a day! Well, I declare! Well, you're not asking much, are you? Now hop off, son, that's the boy, and have a play, and let daddy do his work."

He hopped off. See See and Barnabas had come along to listen in, and away the three of them went. Down the path, over the culvert, around past the well, over to See See's house, pulling imaginary motor cars. Too-too-tooing loud enough to be heard everywhere. Before long, however, the work under supervision absorbed father so completely that by breakfast time he had almost forgotten the motor car.

Two beaming faces met him at the table. "What a good boy Lenny has been!" said mother. "He's eaten two nice plates of porridge," and Lenny added, "I good boy, daddy. You make good boys motor cars? Daddy, you going to make a motor car for me in a day?"

"Oh, son," groaned tired daddy, "motor car again! Can't you give that motor car a rest?" But that was too deep for Lenny. He thought it must be some kind of ride or something, so chattered on. "Yes, daddy, and See See a ride, and Barnabas. Will it have two seats, daddy? and a too-too like a train; an' paint it green, huh, daddy?"

"But, son, how can daddy make you all this big motor car? Where are the wheels?" But once more he ignored my question, feeling that that was all my business. It had nothing to do with him. "But you said, daddy. You said you is going to make me a motor car."

"All right! All right! son, I'll make you twenty motor cars, but keep quiet and let me have some breakfast." In a minute his meal was finished and away he went, again to conference with See See and Barnabas to arrange a program of pulls and rides. In the meantime father and mother had a chance to breathe, and mother said, "Of course you know you could have the old go-cart wheels."

And as father ate, his heart burned. Oh, how he loved this little four-year-old man, who called him, "My great big daddy"! And daddy could remember away back in the years his best and most-loved toy,—a real carved-out boat *his* father had made. Yes, his father had been busy too, but he got the boat made somehow. Anyway, busy is a lame excuse for anything. It's only said when we don't want to do something. Of course there is no time. There never is. But it's wonderful how you can make time when you want to and, well—yes, father would make the boy a motor car, with a too-too like a train, and put a seat in it,

and paint it green.

In between classes in school he laid his plans. After worship at night he got to work, and while Lenny dreamed, father built the motor car with a seat in it and a too-too on it. He mixed the paint with gasoline so that by morning the paint was dry and the big motor car was right beside Lenny's bed.

It was 4:30 A. M. In bumped Lenny to have another confidential chat about the motor car. "But," argued father, "you want daddy to do lots and lots of things for you; you should do lots of things for daddy too."

"Yes, daddy, I make."

"Well, what will you make?"

"What daddy tell me."

"All right, son, jump out and get daddy's boots." And out he jumped,—right into his motor car.

"Oh, daddy, you make for me in a day! I know you make! I know you make! You said you'd make for me a motor car. Oh, look, mummy! My big motor car! Look, mamma! The too-too! and the seat! My big daddy make for me!" Mamma dressed him in it, and helped him down the steps, then off he went to See See's.

And so when I read in the Bible, "If a son shall ask bread of any of you that is a father, will he give him a stone?" if I know anything about fathers, and sons—not even the very good fathers like those we read of in articles, but the very common, ordinary sort that most of us are, as the Bible says, the "being evil" variety, I'd say, "Of course he wouldn't!

1. Healed by the power of the white man's God.
2. "Will yer give me a ride too?"
3. "My daddy's going to make me a motor car!"
4. All angry words forgotten.
5. The jungle dispensary.
6. Ma Thein Nyok after the "burned finger" was cut off.
7. Elephants frequent our dispensary.
8. Chat Nu, the priest feeder, and his family.
9. On the Salween River, Burma.

He'd give him bread, twenty loaves of bread! All the bread he wanted, dear little soul."

If we then being evil know how to give good gifts unto our children, how much more shall our heavenly Father give the Holy Spirit to them that ask Him?

A Sore Leg and a Sore Heart

"See See! Come an' have a game. See See!"

No answer.

"Oh, See See, come an' have a ride in my motor car. Come on. I'll push yer."

No answer. See See had the grumps. He stood on one leg with his back against the bamboo wall, one finger poked aimlessly into his mouth, with the corners turned down, making it plain to every one who saw him that the whole world had gone wrong that day. Yes, and his leg was sore too,—the one he wasn't standing on,—it had a boil on it. But Lenny didn't know that, and he called again, rather impatiently:

"Oh, See See, what's the matter with yer! Come an' have a game."

No answer.

Then: "You nasty thing, not comin' to play wi' me! I won't play wi' yer any more. Come on, See See. Come on!"

No answer.

"Huh, won't even talk t' me! All right, I'll never speak t' yer any more either. Naughty boy! Don't you ever come over t' my place any more! I won't let yer come up th' stairs. Wouldn't come an' play wi' me! Naughty boy! That's what you are."

And I'm afraid Lenny said some more things which I'm too ashamed to write down, for Lenny was angry; and, turning his back on See See's house, he gave the motor car a jerk, and started off down the road. He was offended. See See had insulted him. Here he was going to give him a ride, but See See wouldn't come. He was going to push him too, but See See wouldn't even talk to him. Never mind, he'd—

But there was some shouting around the corner, near the well, and the sluggish footsteps lightened and quickened into a run. The clouds sped away, leaving a happy face with big eyes filled with question marks. It was Barnabas and Joshua playing tops; and Enoch was trying to spin a top, and it wabbled just like an old man! Ha! Ha! Ha! how funny it looked!

"See if ye can spin a top, Lenny!"

And little fingers were soon occupied winding and re-winding string. Such fun they had that Lenny began to think this was the happiest day in all his life. "Now if only See See was here too," and in a twink, all angry words forgotten, he was off to get See See once more.

"He's not home," called his mother, "he's gone to the dispensary to have his leg treated." So off down the street through the granadilla archway, to get See See in the dispensary, went Lenny and the motor car.

Thara Baird was putting some hot stuff on some cotton wool, and See See sniffled a bit when he put it on and bound it on.

"Did it hurt?" asked Lenny, his little heart beating with loving sympathy, but See See couldn't talk, his heart was too full,—and his eyes.

"Poor See See, can't yer walk?"

Thara Baird was finished now, but See See sat there seemingly powerless to move.

"Thara Baird, has he got a sore leg? Can't he walk?" asked Lenny, his voice almost choking with pity. Then fully persuaded of what his duty was, he said, "Never mind, See See, I'll take yer home in m' motor car." And two little arms folded tight around a wounded comrade. Their hearts beat close, and neither knew that the other had ever said an unkind thing in all his life before.

But oh, how heavy See See was! He mustn't let him fall. "Quick, quick, Thara Baird, help me. I want to put See See into my motor car, but he's too heavy." Thara Baird was right at hand, watching the drama with great interest, and the asked-for help, immediate on demand, soon had See See deposited safely on the car, and in a minute off they went, around the dispensary, slowly over the rough places—away down the path through the granadilla arch once more right up to the steps of See See's house. But Lenny couldn't carry him up the steps by himself, so whispering words of encouragement in See See's ear, off he went to the school where See See's father was teaching. "Thara Peter, come quick! See See's got a sore leg, an' I can't carry him up the stairs by myself," said he, and soon See See was safe inside once more.

"When yer leg gets better, will yer come an' play tops wi' me, See See?" But See See's heart was too full, and his eyes, to answer, and it was only after a big effort that he could give his head a big nod. But Lenny understood. He had

forgiven and forgotten and had been forgiven—almost as
quick as it had happened.

And I think that's what Jesus meant when he said, "Except ye . . . become as little children, ye shall not enter
into the kingdom of heaven."

"The Little Woman With a Big God"

THE house was strangely quiet as they approached it.
But for a stray chicken or two scratching near the paddy
pounder, a full-grown sow with a litter of little squawkers,
grazing in the sunshine, and a lone dog barking his chal-
lenge, there were no customary signs of life. No fire in the
fireplace, no one turning the cotton gin, no children playing
around. Indeed, the ladder itself was drawn up and hung
on a floor joist.

"There's nobody home," suggested Mooga.

"Yes, there is,—she's inside," replied the man who had
been looking three or four days for a jungle doctor to treat
his wife, and at last had been directed to the Karen pastor's
wife. "She smells so bad no one will stay with her. We've
offered rice to the spirits, we've sent an offering to the
Phongyi, we have rubbed her with bewitched oil,—nothing's any good,—but if you'll only—" and he unhooked
the ladder for the party to ascend into the house. Mooga
reached for a handkerchief and felt funny all over; they
were not inside yet, but already the cause of the poor patient's loneliness was so manifest that she trembled a little.
Because after all she was only a little woman, she could
easily stand under my outstretched arm; and, sitting down

to compose herself, she waited till the man opened the door and called for her.

"Whatever did you do? Whatever is the matter?" she exclaimed, as she forced herself, in spite of the terrible odor, to the patient's side, and from out of the bundle of disheveled rags and blankets came the trembling, faltering reply: "You know over there near the waterpots, where we throw the refuse, and pour the rice water, and bathe, and underneath where the pigs wallow? Well, on account of the heavy rains the bamboos had rotted, and without realizing it, I was carrying up a heavy waterpot, and while putting it down, the floor gave way and down I went. The cruel ragged splinters of the broken bamboos tore the skin off my legs, and cut my body—oh, how it hurt! And it landed me in all that slime. The pigs fled for their lives, and I was left to pick myself up slowly as best I could. In no time there was a crowd around me, and every one thought it a huge joke—all except me. And by the time I was washed and dressed again, I could almost have forgotten about it,— except I was sore and cut and scraped,—and little thinking, I fried the curry for the evening meal,—and that was the mistake. Now the "fry smell" has gone all through my body, and all those scraped and cut places are loathsome and foul-smelling sores. Please look, and see if you can help me."

It was no time to smile at the poor woman's superstition of the "fry smell." Something must be done. The dirty clothes were slowly removed, revealing the most impossible sight poor Mooga had ever seen. She tried to look, but the terror of it shut her eyes. She tried to touch, but the thought of it made her shudder. "Oh, sister," she said, "what can I do? I dare not touch; I dare not look."

But the pain in those eyes, the disappointment of lost hope in that saddened face, stirred her soul to its depths, and stroking the careworn brow she continued: "I'm only a little woman, I can't do much, but I've got a big God. He knows everything and can do everything. For Christ's sake, I'll ask Him what to do, and then do my best."

Oh, what a glorious thought,—a big God who can do everything! The sickening, foul-smelling room seemed lighted with His presence. The fire was lighted, hot water prepared, the floors swept, the sores washed and dressed with simple ointment. It seemed to take hours, but at last the first treatment had been given. The patient had been bound in clean bandages, and dressed in clean clothes; the dirty blankets were put to soak, and the old rags burned; but Mooga lingered just a moment, to say, "Sister, this is all I can do; but let's ask my big, big God to do the rest," and together they bowed in prayer.

"Outside the reaction came," she afterwards told me. "Oh, how I dreaded to think of the next trip! That night I couldn't swallow my food, because you know I'd never seen anything like it. I'm not even a nurse. All I know is what I've learned in bringing up my own seven. But that taught me to rely on our big God. Really," she said, warming up to the subject, "I've seen God work miracles. Things I couldn't even diagnose have answered to the simplest of treatments. This poor woman was quite well again in about two weeks, and has promised to come to Sabbath school.

"Then you saw that man standing on the steps while we were having meeting last night? Oh, I never saw anyone so swollen in my life. It seemed he must surely burst. Every breath seemed that it must be the last. I made my husband learn to treat the men patients (and you would have thought he was handling snakes when he first started; he was simply frightened of it). But I told him we had a big God on our side, and,—well, we pulled him through.

"Since we have come to this village, the Buddhist priest has moved out,—and we are called upon for everything. I wouldn't dare to take the responsibility by myself; but with our big God, Thara, oh yes, that makes all the difference!"

And Mooga could have talked on for hours, telling of her cases; but seeing the hour was late, and I was tired after a long journey, she left me to retire. And on my knees I breathed a prayer for another jungle hero,—the little woman with the big God.

※⁂※

The Boy Who Dared to Tell Daddy

"Now you catch me, e-e-e-e-h!" and childish mirth rang out till it fairly shook the little mat house where See See and Barnabas were playing. Mother and father had gone out for a little while, and the boys, left in charge, had played at hide and seek, then tag, and now were having a wonderful time at "cat and mouse."

"Now I'll be the cat, and chase you. Quick, look out! There, I've got you!"

"Now, me."

"Quick, run, jump, I'll be on you—" SMASH!

And two little boys turned white and awfully quiet all of a sudden, for they knew something was broken. It was a plate, which had shaken off the shelf, as See See—the mouse—had made a big jump to save himself from being caught.

"Oo—oo—oo! It was your fault!" taunted Barnabas, who could hardly help feeling glad it wasn't he. "Now, daddy will give you a beating. You see if he won't. Then jumping up and down on one leg he teased, "Oh, I know some one who's going to get a beat-ing! I know. I know. I kno-ow! It isn't me. I didn't do it. See See's goin' t' get a whackin'. See See's—" But See, See, summing up the whole situation, had quickly disappeared.

"Where are you, See See? Oh, See See!" But there was no answer, for See See was off down the path as fast as he could go to his daddy. "Oh, daddy," he sobbed, "me an' Barnabas was playin' an'—was just playin' an'—an' a plate fell down an' smashed. Boo-hoo-hoo, I didn't mean to, daddy; I never saw it; I didn't know it would tumble down an' smash. Boo-hoo! Daddy, daddy, are y' goin' to whip me, daddy?" But his daddy, touched with the little fellow's genuine confession, put his hand on his head and said, "Why no, son; it wasn't all your fault; and you've done the best you could by coming and telling me at once. We all have accidents sometimes, and next time you'll be more careful, won't you?"

Magical forgiveness! Heavy heart turned to a heart as light as air. Sorrow turned to joy. Tears gone without a trace, and bounding back home, he joined Barnabas in the frolic once more.

"Where you been?" demanded Barnabas; but that was See See's secret. He knew but he wasn't going to tell. "Never you mind. Let's play under the house this time. Which d' y' want t' be, cat or mouse?" But Barnabas didn't want to be either. He just wanted to jump up and down on one leg and then the other, teasing poor See See.

"Whoo—oo—oo, wait till father comes home! See See's goin' t' get a beatin'," and he made up a little song to fit the words, but couldn't understand why See See didn't get mad.

"Aren't y' scared, See See?"

"Naw."

"But y'll get a whippin'."

"Never mind."

"You jus' wait an' see. Then y' won't say, 'Never mind.' Here, quick, daddy and mamma's coming. Better run and hide." But See See didn't seem one tiny little bit scared, and surprised Barnabas by walking slowly to meet his daddy down the path.

"Oh, daddy, See See broke a pla-ate; See See broke a pla-ate!" blurted Barnabas, then took up his tune accompanied by his one-leg hop-step dance. "See See's going' t' get a whackin-n. See See's—"

"I know all about it," said his father (by this time See See had daddy firmly by the hand, his face showing very vividly that he didn't dread a whacking nearly as much as he hated that tune Barnabas was singing),—"and See See is not going to get any whacking. He came and told me first; and I've forgiven him."

Oh, wasn't it worth telling daddy right away! He wasn't the least, tiniest, weeniest bit scared, 'cause his daddy had forgiven him. Dear boys and girls, learn to know the joy of being forgiven. Tell daddy and mamma all about it. It's wonderful how they can understand, when we tell them; and, better still, this is the way we learn to confess our sins to God and to know the beautiful joy of His forgiveness.

{ 65 }

3—J.H.

The Jungle Man's Prayer

"Oh, Thara! Quick! One of my men has been 'stung' by an elephant. Oh, do come!" panted a stalwart son of the jungle as he came rushing into my office, where I was working at my desk one evening. His hair was all matted, and his work-soiled clothes disheveled. But his veins, standing out with fatigue, the perspiration rolling down his face, his eyes wild with fear, added an irresistible earnestness to his appeal.

One cannot live for twelve years among such people without learning to read them at a glance, so, spending no time in useless formalities, but springing to my feet, I asked, "Where is he?"

"In a canoe at the river bank," he answered, as we left the house.

"And where was he stung?"

We were going too fast for proper conversation, but pointing to his thigh, he simply said, "Here."

"Were his bowels hurt?" I asked again, suspiciously.

He gave no answer, but pushed his way through the grass and the reeds to the river. "There," he said, "look for yourself;" and I looked.

There was a small canoe, some twenty feet long, that would hold about eight people, and lying on some bamboos near the center lay the unfortunate man. I was by his side in a moment. His pale face, tense lips, and heavy breathing lent a seriousness to the situation which reached a ghastly climax when I lifted the blanket to find the poor man's bowels all outside and wrapped up in his dirty loin cloth. He had been gored in the abdomen by his elephant.

A little bunch of boys had followed us down, so, sending one for a lamp, one for the school blackboard to serve as a stretcher, and another for Brother Baird, I busied myself with a further hasty examination, listening the while to a tale that would make your heart sick. They told of this certain elephant's killing a man last year. His tusks had been depointed for that, and two men had been put on him. This day, being in a nasty mood, the elephant became infuriated as his drivers tried to urge him to pull out a certain chain; he had knocked one of the men down, and gored him. The man was thought to be dead, and no wonder, for what could look more like death than a disemboweled man lying in his gore? But seeing he still lived, they made a bamboo bed and brought him twenty miles to our dispensary,—four long hours in the hot sun! And what kind of hospital had we to care for such a case? Only a rough but neat wooden building, sawed and built by the schoolboys, where, no doctor being available, missionary nurses dispense healing and comfort as they are able. There was not another hospital for sixty miles around; so we had no alternative but to receive him and do what we could.

We had a few ounces of ether among our medicines which we kept for making toothache drops and diluting our collodion. And soon the wounded man was fast asleep on our little operating table. Brother Baird then carefully washed the bowels in sterile saline solution and, putting them back in place, sewed up the wound as best he could. We then bound him up, and waited anxiously for him to come to. It didn't take long. A look of fright, a groping for the bowels, a tired smile, and he struggled to rise, saying, "Now let me go home."

"But, brother!" we said, "unless the God of heaven works a miracle for you, you never will go home," and we had to tell him earnestly how serious his case was. Hopeless, yes, hopeless, so far as we could see; but we said, "Brother, when we have done our best, we always ask God to do the rest. We are going to pray. If you are able, you pray too." Then Brother Baird prayed and I prayed—not that our case would pull through, but that if God could use this man's recovery to honor His name and cause, He would graciously give us his life. Then the poor jungle man prayed. Oh, such a prayer! Short, simple, and earnest.

"God of the white man, make me better!
God of the white man, make me better!"

And the God of the white man heard that jungle man's prayer.

Miracle? It was! For in five days those bruised tissues began to slough away. By ten days every stitch we put in had rotted out, and we could see one loop of the bowel at the widest part of the gash, where also the most offensive-smelling pus was coming away in cupfuls. What could we do? What could anyone do? Brother Baird cleaned the wound night and day, and we prayed. And we saw those muscles grow and stick on to the bowel, then cover it. Then the skin closed in, little by little, and in two and a half months that man walked thirty-eight miles to his home, well and strong. And he is still alive and working hard,— a living witness to the power of the God of the white man.

The Burned Finger

THERE they stood, around the verandas, on the steps, crowded into the reception hall. Indians, Burmese, jungle Karens; inpatients, outpatients, friends, and curious on-lookers; skin-diseased, sore-eyed, fever-racked, sick, and dying. It was the only dispensary for sixty miles north or south, and there is no way of measuring the distance east or west. Brother Baird and his assistants were busy as only jungle missionaries can be, when—

"Oh, Thara, won't you come to see my daughter?" pleaded a kind-faced old man. "She's burned her finger."

"All right, uncle, in just a little while; we've nearly finished here for this morning." And before long, a little bottle of picric acid and a few bandages in his bag, he went with old uncle by launch to his village to see the poor girl.

"Last year," explained the father, with trembling lips, as they neared the house, "she had a fit, and fell with a lamp, setting fire to the baby's bed. Before we could get to the scene and put out the flames, the little one was burned to death; and now she has had another fit and fallen into the fire, and burned her finger."

They went up the ladder into the house, where Brother Baird saw a young woman lying on the floor. She had truly fallen into the fire and burned her finger; but, no one being near at the time, before she could come to, and pull her arm from the fire, it had burned the fourth and fifth fingers right off and all the flesh from the under side of the arm, uncovering the ulna bone almost to the elbow. And then, because they knew no better, and because the father was away from home at the time, the poor girl lay on her mat, the arm uncared for and uncovered. It had been in this condition for fifteen days, the flies had blown the rotting mass, and the maggots were eating the poor girl alive. And Brother Baird had a little bottle of picric acid with which to tackle the job!

"Take her to the hospital, and have it cut off," he pleaded. But the hospital was sixty miles away,—sixty jungle miles, which might take from two to four days for a sick person to travel, and we knew she could never live to get there. "Oh, Thara, won't you cut it off," they pleaded in reply. "We can't take her to the hospital; and if you don't do it, she must die!" Too well we knew it; but oh, how serious a thing to be the only one between the poor sufferer and death! Yes, he must do his best; so he brought the patient to our little jungle dispensary, where at once all was astir, sterilizing, preparing bandages and pads and the few little instruments that we had. Soon we were ready, white-clad, and confident. There followed a short prayer and the operation.

An hour and a quarter later the patient groaned, half opened her eyes, and wanting to turn, groped with the other hand to ease over the member of death,—but it wasn't there! She groped again, and opened her eyes a little wider. For a moment she was startled with fear, and, lifting her head, groped again. The pathetic picture brought tears to our eyes. "Is it finished already?" she asked, and smiling dropped off to sleep.

Twenty-nine days later: Ma Thein Nyok went home with the bandages off, her life saved, and she had experienced the power of the missionaries' God.

Chat Nu the Priest Feeder

"Ho, Uncle Thara! Where have you come from?"

"Oh, brother, just from over there. Where've you come from?"

"From over there too! What are you doing?"

"Just buying a few things in the market. What are you doing?"

"I'm just buying a few things in the market too! When you've finished, where are you going?"

"When I've finished, I'm going home. Where are you going?"

"Oh, when I'm finished, I'm going home too."

Thus did Chat Nu the priest feeder greet Evangelist Tha Myaing one fine day in the bazaar of the town of four banyan trees.

And thus did our evangelist return the greeting. Not that either was inquisitive concerning the other's business. For this is the way we say good day and good morning in the jungle. The greeting being now over, however, the questioner continued.

"Yes, but after you have gone home, Thara, then what are you going to do?"

"Oh! Now,—then,—I am going to make preparation to go to the Kamamaung camp meeting."

"The Kamamaung camp meeting? Fine! May I come too?"

"Sure, you may come too."

"What day are you going?"

"Tuesday."

"Fine! What train are you riding?"

"The 12:30 at noon."

"Fine! I'll be there," and turning, Chat Nu quickly disappeared in the crowd.

Tha Myaing looked intently after him. "I've never seen him before," he thought to himself. "How talks he of coming to camp meeting! Would that his words were true;" but, knowing how easy it is to talk in the jungle, he forthwith promptly forgot the incident, finished his purchases, and went home.

At last Tuesday came. The camp meeting preparations were completed, and by 11:30 our evangelist was walking up and down on the station platform with his wife, waiting for the train to come, when "Ho, Uncle Thara!" called a big voice behind him. Turning, what was his surprise to find the friend of the market experience a few days before, coming toward him, grinning all over, and evidently quite pleased with everything in general.

"Well, here I am," he said.

"Yes. But where are you going?"

"Didn't you say I could come with you to the camp meeting?"

"Yes. Well, where's your ticket?"

"Oh, all right, then, I'll get my ticket," and returning from the ticket office in a few minutes with a brown ticket marked Moulmein, he said, "Now may I come?"

Tha Myaing eyed his friend with more astonishment than ever.

"Now, brother," he said seriously, "you're a man, and I'm a man. Let us not play with our words. You don't know me, and I don't know you. How, then, is it that you are coming to the camp meeting?"

1. Called together for prayer.
2. "This is *our* house," Mg Thein told his father.
3. The Jungle Band.
4. The school Mg Thein attended.
5. Band music at camp meeting at Awbawa.
6. Mg Thein's father did not object to his son's learning to work and to study.
7. Uncle from the hills goes to camp meeting at Awbawa.

"Oh, now, Uncle Thara! That's my secret. You don't know me, but I know you! Don't you remember such-and-such a time you were talking with Mr. Po Thein in Mawney village?"

"Yes, I do."

"And you talked so long that it got dark and you couldn't go home that night?"

"Yes."

"And Po Thein said, 'Never mind, I have a friend here who will be glad to have us sleep in his house.' So he took you up into his friend's house, and, sitting down on the mats, he lit a lamp, and you talked and talked some more?"

"Yes, I recall it all."

"Well, that was my house. I was out in the field when you came, and I was surprised to hear voices in my front room when I came home. I listened downstairs, and soon recognized it was a preacher. I don't like preachers. Don't know how it is. They never have appealed to me. I've spent all my life feeding Buddhist priests and building Buddhist temples, and I kind of felt I had enough merit stored up to last me, so I went quietly up the back steps, cooked my rice in the kitchen, and after eating it, lay down on a mat beside the fire. But you and Po Thein were on the other side of the wall, and you were preaching, preaching, preaching. I couldn't go to sleep. I just had to listen. You preached till nine o'clock, then ten o'clock, then eleven o'clock, and finally, about midnight, you rolled over and went to sleep. But by this time I couldn't sleep. I had heard so much that I was all awake inside. You had been talking about the peace of God in our hearts—a peace which the world could not understand, and I realized that all my life that was the peace that I had longed for, and all my priest feeding hadn't given it to me. You had pleaded with Po Thein to come and attend the Kamamaung camp meeting. You told him he would find this wonderful peace and joy there. Before morning I determined that I should get there too. So now, Uncle Thara, I have my ticket; what else do I have to do?"

"I could tell you something to do, brother," said Tha Myaing's wife, seeing that her husband was still too astonished to speak.

"Well, what can it be? Speak!"

"You know Adventists don't smoke; and you ought to give up smoking if you're coming to the camp meeting."

"Oh, all right," he said.

"Can you do without your pipe for five days?"

"Auntie Tharamoo, by that will I know it. Did not Uncle Thara say the Christ was powerful to save and to keep? If what he says about the peace of God is true, He will help me give up the tobacco, surely." And, going over to the iron fence of the station, he stuck his pipe on the top of one of the pickets, and, emptying his pockets of all the tobacco he had, he placed it on the ground at the bottom of the picket as if making an offering to some evil spirit.

"Come and see! Come and see!" he called. "God helping me, this is the end of my sacrifices to devils."

The rest of the story is easily told. All that day as they traveled by train, they talked and studied. All the next day as they traveled up river by the little steamer, they talked and studied. Then for five days he drank in the truth, till he found the peace of God and had accepted Christ. Among the first he stood, as the call was made for those who wanted to accept Christ to rise. We wrote his name down in the

"Little Brothers' " class. And he went back home with his face shining and his heart pulsating with a joy he had never known before.

Three months later I visited him. His face still shone. His mouth was clean. I needed not to ask, but I did say, "Did you ever go and see if the old pipe was where you left it on the old picket fence?"

"No, sir!" he said. "From that day to this I've never touched the filthy stuff, and God helping me I never will."

A few more months and he and his eldest daughter were baptized, and the other children were put in school. Chat Nu, the priest feeder, had been born again into Chat Nu the Christian.

The Band in the Jungle

(WITH APOLOGIES TO WOODWORTH)

How dear to my heart are the scenes of the jungle
    When fond recollection presents them to view!
The people contented in dark superstition
    To live and to die. 'Twas all that they knew.
We longed, how we longed, to preach them the gospel,
    To teach them the truth that we all hold so dear,
But, 'fraid of the white man and all that came with him,
    They fled in confusion whene'er he drew near.
We tried and we tried to preach them the gospel;
    But what can you do when they're governed by fear?

We took them the pictures, the magic night pictures;
    We cared for the sick and bound up their sores;
By blowing our cornets, we called them together,
    And soon had a meeting. And this is the cause:

The boys all declared that they wished they had cornets
　　To help preach the gospel to great and to small.
To Australia's fair land, our Thara went on furlough,
　　And told there the story,—the jungle boys' call:
They wanted some cornets to help spread the message,
　　And win souls to Jesus who died to save all.

The folks in the homeland were touched with the pleading,
　　The one gave a trumpet, and one gave a drum,
And one sent a check, and another a trombone,
　　And in a few months the whole thing was done.
Six cornets, a eupho, and two E-flat basses,
　　Two tenors, four trombones, a new baritone.
We packed them in boxes—in iron-bound boxes—
　　And sent them to Burma—a long way from home—
To the boys in the jungle, who wanted some cornets
　　To help preach the gospel where'er they might roam.

A band in the jungle! A brass band with cornets!
　　The news spread abroad to those governed by fear,
And uncles and aunties, and nieces and nephews,
　　And grandmas and grandpas came running to hear.
The drum beat enthralled them. The beautiful music
　　Was sweeter to them than their dirges so drear.
They now dared to listen to singing and preaching,
　　To tales of the gospel proclaimed far and near;
And some came to church, and some sent their children.
　　The band in the jungle had conquered their fear.

Up mountain and valley, 'cross rivers and streamlets,
　　Away went the band with its message of cheer.
The road was oft dreary, and rough was the pathway,
　　But on marched the band with Thara in the rear.
Oft split were the basses, oft dented the cornets,
　　Or lost was a valve cap, or broken a spring;
But there in each village, their courage still flying,

The cracks stopped with soap, and the joints tied with
    string,
The band in the jungle, without the least grumble,
    To poor, waiting people its message would bring.

How dear to my heart is the band in the jungle!
    The dear boys that play it through thick and through
    thin,
With all of its noise, and all of its jumble;
    Its cornets all soldered and patched up with tin;
The sore feet, and blisters, the marches at nighttime,
    To miss the hot winds and the dust by the day;
At night when I kneel at my bed and am praying,
    All rush to my memory, and lead me to say,

Oh, Lord, bless the band, the band in the jungle;
    And bless the dear boys who blow it alway.
And when the old cornets, the patched-up old cornets,
    Are worn out and useless and thrown away,
Lord, gather the souls the boys have been winning
    By blowing the band in the jungle, I pray.

The Jungle Bandmaster Loses
His Cornet

"One, two, three, four, five, six, seven, eight."

"Hold on, porter, there's one more piece,—a basket."

"No, sir! Your ticket says eight pieces. That's all you put in."

"But the basket! It's got my cornet in it, porter—"

"Well, I'm very sorry for you, mister, but it isn't usual to expect more out of a cloakroom than you put in. You'd better inform the police."

"Inform the what?"

"Inform the police."

"Then is it really, truly lost?"

The realization of the awful truth, the mental checking up only to find the porter's statements correct, made me dizzy. No, stopping to think, I couldn't remember seeing the basket when we got off the train in the morning. I may as well confess to start with that I'm the jungle bandmaster, and though it doesn't sound nice to tell a story about one's self, yet it can't be helped this time. I'm the one that lost his cornet, and oh, how sick I felt over it all!

Here we were on our way to the Taikgyi meeting. The good pastor there wanted some help with the music, but now it was gone. Gone! The cornet that I had been playing for fifteen years—gone! The cornet that had inspired the jungle band, and had played in a hundred villages,—GONE! I've seen some disheartened people in my life, but if ever you come across a sicker-looking individual than a jungle bandmaster who has lost his cornet, then I don't want to meet him.

I informed the police. I informed the station master, and searched the station and the "lost luggage" room. I asked every coolie within hearing distance, if he had seen my basket. Of course there was only one basket. There could only ever be one basket, and that was the basket which had my cornet in it. But not a soul had seen such a basket all day long. Neither had I. That was just the whole trouble. The basket was lost, I tell you, and my cornet was GONE!

Lifelessly I put my eight pieces of luggage into the *gharry,* and directed the *gharry-wallah* to the mission house. Even had the hour of death been nigh, I could not have felt more hopelessly dejected than I did then, till my soul reacted with the thought of prayer. Why, of course! Man's extremity,—God's opportunity,—that sounded brighter. Why not pray? So right there in that old *gharry*, rumbling off down the road, mingling with the thousand sounds and voices common to an Eastern street,—I prayed, —a real prayer.

I told the Lord that that cornet was just as much His as it was mine. I told the Lord that it was just as good a preacher as I was; then as we talked the situation over together, I dared to ask Him, that if it could glorify His name, if it could benefit His cause, to please have it sent back that evening, as I wanted to take it to the Taikgyi meeting the next day.

Talking it all over with the Lord lifted my burden and gave me the assurance that God was now going to take matters into His hands. Maybe He would teach me a severe lesson. But I felt safe in the hands of the Lord, because He always works things out for our good in the long run, and in this frame of mind I completed the journey to the mission house, where my wife, sharing my disappointments and hopes, helped me get things ready for the night.

We were still fixing our camp cots and putting up the mosquito nets, when about five o'clock there was a knock on the door, and a Mr. Minus, a total stranger to us, stood there, asking for "Mr. Hare."

"Mr. Hare," he said, "excuse me, but was your wife traveling on the Maulmein train last night?"

"Yes!" I blurted out, holding my breath.

"Well, a friend of mine was in the same—"

"Have you got my cornet?" I interrupted.

{ 81 }

"I don't know what I've got, but if you'll come and—"

"It was in a basket with some rugs and pillows," I called out, as I dashed out to his *gharry*.

"Well, that's it," he said.

And the next minute I was happy, repossessed of my cornet, and speechless for just a moment.

"My friend has been after me all day to try to hunt you up," he explained at last. "But I didn't have much hope of finding you in this big city. But at last, at half-past three, I could stand it no longer. She knew the name was Hare from the reservation ticket on the carriage. She knew you were Seventh-day Adventists from the conversation she had had with your wife. So I traced you from the church to the pastor's house, then to the office, then here. The basket got mixed up with her luggage somehow. I do hope it has not caused you any inconvenience."

"What time did you start from your home?" I asked.

"About half-past three."

Something seemed to well up big in my heart as I remembered that it was just half-past three that I was talking it all over with the Lord as the old *gharry* went rattling down the busy road.

⁂

Over the Hills and Far Away

THE band boys knew it was planned for them to go by train to the annual meeting at Awbawa, and this fact itself, to say nothing of the brand-new black trousers and white shirts for uniform, had almost threatened to spoil the final examinations. But little had they dreamed of the serious talks the Rangoon church pastor and their Thara had had together, planning to request the committee to permit of a forty-eight-mile detour, to give the Rangoon friends some jungle music. Such things naturally take time; but now the plan had been sanctioned, and the news was out.

"Eh! Going to Rangoon?"

"Yeh! Thara said so."

"All of us?"

"So I hear."

"When?"

"Soon as school's closed."

And the little second-cornet player, intoxicated with such sudden anticipation of delight, rushed around to all the band boys, telling and asking, both together, all at once, to make sure that everybody knew, and also to be sure that his ears had heard right.

The next week, outside of examinations, saw little else than practice, brass polish, and preparation.

We had already, in anticipation of our trip, run all the instruments through the repair shop, fitted a new drumhead to each drum, put in six new springs, fixed four water keys, put corks in three others because they were hopeless, straightened out two dented bells, soldered up two cracked seams, and made four lyres,—but that was easy.

We selected our program from the tunes we had been playing during the year, and rehearsed and rehearsed. I noticed that at the rehearsal just eight days before our departure my solo E-flat bass player was absent. He was one of my teachers, and had one or two very prominent parts. On making inquiry, we found his wife sick, so sick that he absolutely could not hope to think of taking the trip. There was only one possible substitute,—one of our old boys from Nitcha; so the next day a messenger was sent after him, and he put in six hours a day practice during that last week; but even that left me feeling shaky.

Two days before we left, my euphonium player was taken bad with dysentery, but, with immediate treatments, he was fortunately able to leave with us, when at last the jungle band set out for the city. Yes, you imagine quite right when you think that I breathed a sigh of relief as we all boarded our motor launch and started! I breathed two hundred sighs of relief! We were to go to Maulmein by boat, then to Rangoon by train, again by train into the Shwegyin valley, for our Awbawa local meeting, and at last a six days' march over the hills and far away—back home to Ohndaw.

Our first stage took us to Shwegon, where we transferred to the river steamer.

"There are only ten minutes before the steamer leaves, boys; don't attempt to go ashore," I called out, and then left them to get aboard while I went to the post office to look for letters. I was back in five minutes. The whistle blew. The gangplank was pulled up, and we pulled out into the stream. I looked around and prepared to breathe some more sighs of relief. The instruments—the nice, shiny brass instruments—were all stacked nicely on the deck, but there was not a boy to be seen.

"Oh, Mr. Captain, please stop the ship," I implored. "My boys are all ashore," and after a few sweet words, and the promise of a little baksheesh, he put back to the bank again.

"No, I didn't hear—"

"We saw you going—"

"We didn't know—" were the excuses the boys offered, as I rounded them up. Some had to leave half-eaten breakfasts on their plates, but we got the boat.

There were one or two who had never seen a boat; but none of them had ridden on a boat so much that the novelty was worn off, so they had a good time, especially when one of our friends sent aboard about a dozen watermelons, halfway down the river. That's one more thing I've found out a brass band can do besides blow,—eat watermelons.

By four o'clock we arrived at Maulmein; very few had ever been so far away before, and fewer still had ever seen a train before. We had a special carriage reserved, yet, even if I do confess to not feeling too pleased about it, can you wonder that, running back to have a look at them all, after one or two stations, I found one poor boy terribly train-sick with disastrous results, one poor lad minus a ticket, and several others with bad headaches?

However, at six o'clock the next morning we arrived in Rangoon. It was our Big Day. Putting the heavy things in carts, we marched to the mission compound, and were soon getting cleaned up. More sighs of relief when,—

"Thara, three of the boys are down with fever!"

And, of course, one had to be my solo tenor horn, which meant we'd have to eliminate our star piece for the evening. However, "while there's life there's hope. Here, take this medicine to—"

"Oh, Thara, one of the boys has left his cornet home!"

"Left his *what?*"

"His cornet!"

"Yes, and Mya Sein Baw says the snares on the side drum are busted."

Oh, well, never mind what I did or what I said. Let me hurry on, and tell you only that the bandmaster had long, long ago given up carrying such burdens as these alone. We visited the leading music store, bought some snares for the drum, had a nice talk with the manager, who lent us a splendid cornet for the evening, and got back home to find my fever patients eating rice. The time drew nearer, we put on our uniforms, the crowd came, also the Lord Mayor, who was to be chairman for the evening, and we marched to our places, not one missing! The program followed without a hitch, even the bandmaster noticed only two little mistakes, so we were not surprised that the Rangoon folks thoroughly enjoyed it, and gladly donated Rs. 177-8 for the Ingathering Campaign.

The next few days, during the Awbawa meeting, all went smoothly, without a worry, and I was beginning to hope that all the rest of the way was to be clear going. But reports of a rough track across the hills made us send back the big drum and one or two of the fever cases, to return home by train. Our little third cornet player had to go back after the first day's march, and one other had already been called away to see his sick grandma, so that left fourteen of us who resolutely set our faces toward the hills.

The lads did fine. We mapped out our track with our halts carefully to gave us about twelve miles a day.

"Not much," you say.

No, not the first day, or the second; but for six consecutive days, up, up, down, down, up, down,—you take it from us, it's plenty! We know. Especially if your blanket and pack and instrument on your back weigh from ten to thirty pounds.

I should like to tell you about the villages, the bubbling brooks, and the meetings we had, but it would get monotonous. So I'll only tell you about one day,—the day we passed over no man's land,—went over the top, crossed the dividing line between the Toungoo and Salween districts. Do you know why they put district boundaries on top of mountain ranges? We do!

We had slept the night before at Tasuder.

"Oh yes, it's a good road."

"You'll get to Lerdo-Ki by noon."

"Yes, we'll give you two guides." So of course we slept well, and didn't mind in the least being called at 4:30 the next morning. It was a bit early for breakfast, but we would be at Lerdo-Ki by noon.

"Do you want to take some rice with you?"

"Oh no, thanks, uncle; it's too heavy to carry, and we are good marchers. We'll be there at twelve o'clock, anyway. Now, where are our guides?"

No answer.

"Our guides, uncle. Are they ready?"

"Um—er—"

"What's that?"

"Er—um—"

"Eh?"

"They have gone to work!"

"To work!"

"Yes."

"What are they scared of? We'll pay them."

"They don't want money; they are scared to come back by themselves, 'cause there's tigers!"

"Tigers!"

"Yes, six of them.—But here's a man who will take you a bit of the way to the next village, and then it's just one straight road."

So away we went, over the hills and far away. Tigers! Six of them! What did we care? There were fourteen of us, and we all had cornets,—we'd play them a march.

In no time we made the next village, and our guide disappeared.

"What's the matter here?"

"Houses all shut up, leaves put on the ladders!"

Finally one old grandpa appeared from nowhere. "It's because there's sickness over the hills," he explained; "four people died in one day, in the same village, and we want to keep it out of here. But you can find the path easy! No bypaths. Only one path straight up and then straight down. You come to a betel plantation, and the village is on your right."

"Sounds easy enough! What about it, boys?" and the fourteen of us sprang to our feet. Away we went, over the hills and far away. Tigers!—ugh!—six of them!—sickness!—four deaths in one day!—no guide—ugh!

Well, it was a bit rough,—tiptop tiger jungle,—but we got there at 12:30. According to our rule, as soon as the village is sighted, those in front sit down and wait for all to catch up; then we all go in together.

"My, but I'm getting hungry!"

"Well, we are here now—stop your worrying!"

"I was only telling you, so you would know."

"Well, I don't need to be told. I've got plenty of inside information myself," the boys were saying to themselves as I brought up the rear.

"All right! Every one here? Come along," and all together we made for the first house. But it looked strange!
No pigs, no children, no ladder.

"Eh?"

"What? The next house just the same? and the next?"

"Empty! Deserted!"

"Oh, dear!"

"Well, that doesn't make my hunger any the less."

"Nor mine either."

"Wish we had carried some rice. It wouldn't have been
much heavier."

But we were all jungle *wallahs,* and we were not over-
excited at finding the village deserted. It's a very common
thing for these bamboo villages to be moved to an opposite
hill. All we had to do was to find it. That's all!

We put our bundles by a little stream, and left the boys
who were too tired to watch them while six of us scouted
out in three directions to find the village. The first one to
find it was to come back and start the band; then we'd all
come back.

But the band didn't start up. In an hour we were all
back,—not a sign of a village anywhere.

"Hum! Well, now what are you going to do?"

"Same as you."

"Well, what's that?"

"Ask me!"

It was too bad, but what could we do? Yet we had to
do something.

"Well, let's have a rest, and think." So we did. The hungry ones picked tender grass and leaf buds, and chewed
them up with onions (we carried a few onions each). One

cut a wild banana stalk and, chopping it open, ate that. But it was no good. He was more hungry than ever. We were all hungry. We older ones were tougher, and didn't show it so much, but it was awful to watch the younger ones snatching at grass and leaves to eat. Poor boys! I can see them yet.

It was now 2:30 P. M., and we would surely have to do something. So once more six of us scattered out in different directions to find anything at all. A path! Something to eat! Anything!

I've told you already, haven't I, that the bandmaster doesn't carry these burdens alone?

In half an hour we were all back. My mate and I had found a boy, so scared that he ran off into the jungle, but he told us the village was moved three miles down the track, and showed us the beginning of the path. Tha Myaing and his mate found a man and a dog, and brought them to our camp. He was so sorry for us that he willingly consented to take us to the village, and though it took us two and a half hours to crawl those three miles, we got there and had, oh, such a meal! We had a good meeting in the morning also (we were too exhausted to wriggle in the evening), and by nine o'clock we were on our way to the next village. We marched only three miles that day, but we were over the top. The path became bigger and clearer, the villages closer and closer together, and after three more uneventful days we were home. All honor to the heroes of the jungle brass band!

"The tigers?"

"Oh, I don't know. We didn't see any!"

Uncle From the Hills Attends His First Meeting

"You know that man, Tha Myaing? Well, I heard him talking around in our village about a meeting they were going to have in Awbawa, and he said they were going to have a brass band there with twenty-one instruments. He talked so much about that meeting and that band that I says, 'Well, I'll see when the moon's up eight days, and if the fever isn't eating anybody, I'll just go down and have a look. It'll only take one day to walk, and I'll stop there one day, and one day to come back.'

"Well, when the moon was up eight days, everybody was quite all right, so I took my pipe and my betel-nut box and put it in my bag, and, picking up my big long knife, away I went.

"When I got to the village, everybody was talking about that band, and I says, 'Where is it?'

"And they says, 'Down there near the school. Come on, we'll take you.'

"But I says, 'No fear! It'll see me! Wait till it's dark.'

"And they laughed and they says, 'It won't eat you.'

"But I says, 'Never mind, I'm too tired just now; I will go later on.' And then I lay down to rest a bit.

"My, but the way those people talked! They said there were big ones, and little ones, and pulling-in-and-out ones, and a drum. Ah, they said it was the sweetest drum they ever heard, and just then I could hear that drum. It sounded as if they were all getting ready to start. So I sneaked around the back of the village and came in gradually behind it. I saw three people under a paddy barn that was about three feet off the ground, so I sneaked under that with them, and there I could see it all. Twenty-one of them in black pants and white shirts, with shining brass horns. Sure, there were big ones and little ones, and fat ones and thin ones. And there was a white man there too.

"My, but I was glad I could be under that paddy barn! What if that white man looked at me! There was a kind of grass shelter erected. It was very big, and there were over two hundred people in it, waiting for the thing to start. While I was waiting, I got a good wad of betel nut ready to chew, and had a good look around. There were lots of other folks kind of shy of this brass band, just like me. Some were behind a fence, there were half a dozen in a wood pile, and behind every tree there were as many as there could be.

"Well, just then that white man said something, and all those boys got very quiet and looked serious. Me, too, I held my breath! It looked like everybody else was holding his breath too. Then that white man's hand moved up and down once or twice, and that whole thing started. The big ones, the little ones, the pulling-in-and-out ones, the drums —everything. They were all playing different, yet it was all together just the same, and nobody could move till that band stopped for a rest. I couldn't even chew my betel nut. I didn't even know it had rolled out of my mouth, till the band stopped, and I knew I'd lost it. They say none of those boys chew betel. No wonder! I couldn't either while they were playing. My, but I was glad I was under the paddy barn! The man next to me says, 'How do you suppose those boys swallow those pulling-in-and-out things, without straightening out their throats?' But I says, 'I don't know. Do they really swallow them?'

"After a little they started off again, and ah me, it was lovely! And every time they played, I felt it was nicer and nicer. I didn't want them to stop. I didn't want to go home any more. I didn't want to eat rice any more.

"Then after a while that white man stood up all by himself. My, but I was scared! How glad I was I was under the barn! But the next minute he was telling us a little story in our own words. Well, I'd never heard tell of a white man like that before, and he said, once when he was a little boy a dog bit him, and ever after that he didn't like dogs, and he wouldn't have one in the house. But one day his little boy brought home a little black dog. Still he didn't like dogs, and he told his little boy he would have to send it away. But his little boy loved that little black dog, and used to share his dinner with it, and his milk with it, and sometimes he used to take it to bed with him; and after a while, just because he saw how much that little son of his loved that little black dog, he says, 'All right, we'll keep him.' And he's had that little black dog ever since, and he wouldn't even sell him now for any price. Then he says that's the way it was with us. God had a Son that He loved very much. His name was Jesus; and Jesus came and shared our food and shared our houses and lived with us for three and a half years, and Jesus loves us so much that God says, 'All right, I'll save every man and woman and child who will show that they love You by obeying You.'

"Well, I never heard of that before. But I reckon that's right. Then the band played some more, and Tha Myaing preached some more, and the next day they did it three times. I thought I was going home the next day after that, but the band was so nice, and you should have heard that white man telling about when he was a little boy. All the things he said and did, and what his mother did. And every time he'd say, 'And that's just the way it is with us and God;' and sure so it was. We could all understand it. I wasn't scared of that band after the first night, and once I sat right up next to the drum. And I found out the boys didn't swallow the pulling-in-and-out slides. It was like a little bamboo inside a big bamboo, moving in and out.

"Oh, I'll never forget that brass band, and that white man telling about when he was a little boy, and how it is just the same with us and God, 'cause so it is."

Disowned for Christ

I CAN see them now. Three little brothers, standing timidly in my office with their father, who had brought them to school. I wrote their names down in the register. Maung Thein, fourteen years old; Aung Thein, ten; Aung Twe, nine. I was still musing on their names and ages when, "What are the school fees, Thara?" asked the father.

"Twenty rupees each; that will make sixty rupees for the three, uncle," I replied.

"Fine," he said, and, putting his hand into the big bag he carried on his shoulder, he produced sixty solid silver rupees, and placed them on my desk.

And with eyes glistening, I said, "Good stuff!" You know I like cash in advance, don't you? It's good business, and I like it.

"And how much do you estimate their books and clothes will cost for the year, Thara?" again asked the father. Now

I can estimate very well under such circumstances, and it didn't take me long to say, "About forty-five rupees, uncle."

"Fine!" he said, and into that same bag went his hand again, and he produced forty-five more silver rupees, and put them on my table. And once more I said to myself, "Good stuff!" And I marked "Paid in advance" by the names of the three brothers, and determined to follow their progress closely. They were good-looking lads. The father was a good-looking man. Almost at once I could feel myself expecting more of them than of the average lad. They had paid cash in advance. It was good business.

A school of this kind was new to them. The regular program, the work, the classes, the silent study hours, the drill, the singing, the brass band. How different it all was from the irregular, noisy, monotonous singing of the Buddhist temple, the only school that they had ever known. But they put their whole heart and soul into everything; and when the first vacation came, what wonderful stories they took home to their village! They had learned some words of the white man's language. The little boys had been making bricks in the brick-making class; and the big boy, who had been in the building class, gave a demonstration of his prowess by making his father a chair.

A chair! The village folk could hardly imagine such a thing. Mg Thein, who had never handled a plane or a saw or a hammer before, had made his father a chair! And they crowded around to admire that chair and to pat it and stroke it. And if there was one thing that father loved doing more than anything else it was to sit in that chair.

The boys came to school another year, and during the second vacation Mg Thein made his father a table!—A table! and again the village folk crowded around to admire the table, and to stroke it and pat it. And if there was anything that father loved doing more than sitting in the chair his boy had made it was to sit in the chair near that table! And the boys came back to school for another year. And during the third year one day the father and mother came up to visit the school, and the boys took them around the mission compound. I was just coming back from the dispensary where I had been treating a patient, and passing near them in front of the boys' house, when—

"This is *our* house," I overheard Mg Thein telling his father. "*We* built it. The two little fellows helped to make the bricks, and I was one of the carpenters," and I could see his chest poking out with legitimate pride as they stood for a moment and examined the beautiful building. And once more I said to myself, "Good stuff!" Do you know, I like to hear people talking about "*our* school" and "*our* message" and "*our* work." It puts the right vision in their eyes. They are "*our* missionaries" and "*our* preachers" and "*our* boys." It's good business,—colaborers, and partners together with God,—and I like it.

Soon, however, the parents' happiness gave way to perplexity at the stories of Christianity the boys brought home. Then, to fear, as the boys showed their unwillingness to partake of the devil feasts, and to join in the worship of the yellow-robed Buddhist priests. And then, to anger, as after four years of school Mg Thein came home one day to ask his father for permission to be baptized.

"That's not what we sent you to school for," raged the angry parents. "To get baptized! huh! the idea! What shame we would have to eat!"

"If you want to get baptized, I'll baptize you myself," said his father. "Next year you shall stop home from school, and plant paddy with me, and I'll baptize your arms and legs in mud. That's the kind of baptism you need." And it was only after much promising and pleading that a compromise was reached, and Mg Thein came back to school alone.

"I've promised my mother and father that I won't be baptized this year, Thara," he explained. "It was the only way I could get back to school, and I can still keep in the Little Brothers' Class, can't I?" I encouraged him as well as I could, promising to pray much, and assuring him that if he lived up to all the light he knew, the Spirit of God would speak to him very plainly, and tell him what to do.

The year went by. The local meeting at the new year drew near. The father and mother came again to visit. But the light had gone out of their faces, and only the anger of evil spirits was visible there.

"Won't you have a talk to dad and mum?" pleaded Mg Thein. And that night we invited them into our house. We had some music, a little refreshment, and chatted pleasantly enough about rice and bullocks. But by and by the atmosphere changed as I said, "Uncle, I would like to talk to you about Mg Thein. You know he is a good lad, and God is moving on his heart to become a Christian."

You've been in a cave and put out your light and felt the darkness, haven't you? The darkness is so dense that it seems you can actually feel it with your fingers. In the same way, you can feel the presence of evil spirits. And this evening I was conscious that these poor people were surrounded by evil angels. My words seemingly went no farther than my lips. They made no sign that they either heard or understood, and after a moment, without a word of greeting, they turned their backs and left our house. Nor did they greet anyone else, nor partake of a parting meal, but left sullenly and angrily for their home.

A few more weeks, and the local meeting came, and on the Friday evening, when the call was made for those who wanted baptism to stand, Mg Thein stood among the first.

"You know, your father hasn't given his permission for your baptism, Mg Thein," I said as I came to him during the examination of the candidates. "And though you have waited your year, it will likely mean that you must stand alone. Do you feel, Mg Thein, that you can stand alone?"

"No, Thara, I don't," was his quick reply. "I am very weak, but the Saviour I have found here at school is strong. He promises to be with me always. If Paul could do all things through Christ, cannot I?"

Oh, friends, can anyone withhold water, that such a young man, with such faith in his Saviour, should not be baptized? So the next day, among the other precious candidates, Mg Thein was baptized. It was a happy day for us. We stood on the river bank, singing "Happy day," but away down in Mg Thein's village, the powers of darkness were at work, and the next morning, at six o'clock, a messenger arrived, bearing a note from the father.

"We hold the devil feast to-night. We require your presence with us," it said.

"What shall I do, Thara?" asked Mg Thein, holding the note before me. "I cannot partake of the devil feast any more. I'm a Christian."

"Write a nice little note and tell dad all about it," I suggested. And he did. He wrote a letter that would soften the heart of almost any parent; but it had no effect on the enraged father in the village, and the next day there arrived two messengers from his village. One told him his mother had lost her reason, and had seized a rope and rushed into the jungle to try to hang herself. The other handed him another note from his father, and Mg Thein paled as he read,

"This baptism cannot be.
It must be undone,
It must be turned inside out
And disannulled.
We hold the devil feast to-night.
You must be here."

Yes, he must go, but we could not let him go alone. So Brother Baird, my associate missionary, went with him to pray and give counsel.

How I would like to describe that scene, as we could picture it after their graphic description; but words seem powerless to paint such hellishness. Even while nearing the house, they were seen, and the cry arose: "Mg Thein's come! He's come!" Almost at once they noticed a figure spring from the house with a rope and rush for the jungle. "It's mother! She's gone to hang herself! Help!" cried some of the sisters, and several gave themselves to the chase. Meanwhile the remaining sisters, weeping and moaning, approached their brother with, "It's all your fault! It's all your fault! You've driven your mother mad; and if she commits suicide, we'll call you a murderer!" Meanwhile the crowd gathered, with chorused suggestions: "Why don't you undo it? Yes, why don't you undo it?" and with them came the village witch. Yes, a real witch; we have them over here in the jungle, witches that associate with devils. And in a moment her shrill voice, easily heard above the others, had the floor:

"Don't you remember," she shrieked, "once before when one of our villagers was baptized, and became a God-worshiper, that that night a tiger came right into the village and ate one of his family?"

"Aye, aye," assented the crowd.

"And that's just what will happen this time. It's got to be undone! I tell you! It's got to be undone!" and the crowd joined in the ever-swelling chorus: "It's got to be undone! It's got to be undone!"

Now add it all together,—the weeping, the madness, the accusing, the screeching, and the chorusing,—and you'll know why Brother Baird and Mg Thein were glad enough to escape with their lives, on the pretext of taking back their message to the mission. "In three days we hold the devil feast," called the father, as they began to retrace their steps. "Dead or alive, be here with the baptism business all undone."

There followed three days of prayer at the mission. We all joined in beseeching God's help in this awful moment. And in three days we had the assurance that God was going to be with us. It was clear that I should go to visit the angry parents; so, calling Peter, the evangelist, and one of the big boys for company, we made the trip, down the river by launch, then inland about five miles. We bowed in worship before leaving the launch, asking the angels to go with us, and God's Spirit to go before us, to prepare the way; and God answered our prayers!

"Hullo, uncle."

We had arrived at the house before noon, and found the father and mother alone, looking angry and weary.

"Uh! Oh, it's Thara. Are there just three of you?"

"Oh no, uncle, there's a whole lot of us, only you can just see three of us. The others are angels, and we have come to cheer you up, and the angels will keep the evil spirits away and give you peace of heart."

"Uh! Where's Maung Thein?" again grunted the displeased father.

"He stayed behind," I replied.

And the mother, who had been sitting on the floor, sullenly sifting rice up to this moment, now sat motionless and inert. Did it just happen, or did God plan our visit when most of the villagers were away? There was no furious crowd, and God gave us words. While I talked, Peter prayed; while Peter talked, I prayed. We told them of the love of God, of His wonderful ways in finding out the honest ones who are worshiping God as well as they know how. We reminded the distraught father of the wonderful way he had been led to bring his boys to the mission school, of the things the boys had learned, and pleaded with him to acknowledge this God who was so anxious to lead them all the way.

The father was moved. "Well," he said, "anyway, for appearance's sake, I will cut off his support; and if he wants to keep on worshiping God, he must work his way through school." We were glad enough to hear even a statement like this.

And then, with a cough and a splutter, his mother opened her mouth, and not recognizing our presence in any way or even glancing our way, prayed and cursed and cursed and

prayed as only a heathen mother could do. Such a bitter
prayer—such bitter curses.

"God of the heaven,
God of the earth,
To-day is the full of the moon,
To-day thou will visit the earth,
To-day thou wilt visit the earth,
And walk among the coconut palms,
And walk among the banana trees.
You will see me in my sorrow,
You will see me in my tears,
Because my son is dead,
My eldest son is dead.
God of the forest,
God of the water,
I call upon thee to witness,
Now hear what I shall say.
Whereas I thought I had nine children,
Behold, I have only eight.
For one is gone to heaven,
We can only see his heels.
We want to go to heaven,
But he won't go the same path with us.
No longer is he my son,
No longer am I his mother.
When I hear he is dead and rotten,
And the worms have eaten his eyes out,
May I not be moved to pity,
And call him again my son.
When he hears I am dead and rotten,
And worms have eaten my eyes out,
Let him not return to call me mother."

Oh, Christian young people, there is no bitterness known
more bitter than that of hopeless animism. There are no

curses more awful than the despairing curses of those who know not our God of love.

We rose to our feet, shook hands, commended the parents to the love of Christ, and assured them that we were going to pray every day that God would reveal His love to them, and touch their hearts and give them hope and peace. Then we brought the news back to Maung Thein, "Your parents acknowledge your baptism, but have cast you off as their son."

"What shall I do now?" pleaded Mg Thein.

"Lad, you have done all you can. God must now do what we cannot do, and in some way touch your parents' hearts," I assured him.

"And will God take away the anger of my parents sometime, Thara?"

"I think He certainly will, Mg Thein, if we live right and keep close to Him," I said. And God did. Blessed be His name.

.   .   .   .   .

There remained but a few weeks to the close of school. And our jungle band was invited to Rangoon City to take part in the Uplift Campaign. The news that the jungle boys were to ride the river steamer and the "fire cart" (railway), and were going to the white man's city, where the streets were paved and motor cars and thunder cars went up and down the streets, spread rapidly around the district.

Mg Thein played the trombone in the jungle band, and the above startling news reached the ears of his mother and father. Yes, they had cursed him and disowned him. But never had any of their relatives such honor, to go to the white man's city; and the news caused much pleasant comment among other village mothers, who wished that their sons could go to the city. "And he shall see the zoo, and the ocean ships!" they told her; "and he shall come back seeing more in a few days than we have seen in our lives," and, without realizing it, her heart beat faster as she thought of the honor her son was bringing upon them.

At last the day came. The jungle band embarked on the river steamer, and village by village we touched our way slowly down to Maulmein.

Was it the third village? I noticed a little old lady with two strong boys beside her. I tried to see her face, but it was covered with her hands. I would have thought no more of it, but, as the steamer started off again, Mg Thein came bounding into my cabin.

"Did you see her, Thara? Did you see her?" he said.

"See whom?"

"Why, mother! As the boat came near the shore, I knew her. Her eyes eagerly sought the faces of the band boys as we stood grouped with our shiny instruments, till her eyes caught mine. I looked for just a moment, and saw her lips form the words, 'My son,' and then she covered her face with her hands. But, oh, Thara, I'm so happy! God is doing it! He's doing it!"

And you should have heard that trombone play in Rangoon City! We had a wonderful time, and after a splendid meeting there, and another five days' meeting at Awbawa Outstation, we marched six days over the hills, up and down, in and out, home to our mission station.

Not long after our arrival there was another note for Mg Thein from his father. It read:

"DEAR MG THEIN,
"On the fourth day of the month of May
Your aunt is to be married.
Come and help us with the wedding."
Signed, "YOUR FATHER."

"Shall I go, Thara?" Mg Thein asked excitedly.

"Go, by all means, lad, and God go with you," I replied. And now listen!

On the very night of the wedding festivities, while all their guests were assembled in Mg Thein's house, at 8:20 P. M., May 4, 1930, Burma was shaken by the most severe earthquake yet known in its history. The town of Pegu, a hundred miles across the valleys, but for a few modern buildings and a few wooden houses, was blotted out and two thousand dead lay buried in its crumbled ruins. Our mission station was shaken to the roots, but undamaged. And that house, filled with its wedding guests, also rocked and leaped, and in a moment faces whitened, eyes protruded, and knees knocked together, as screaming voices called out, "What's the matter? What's the matter?"

Mg Thein sprang to his feet in a moment. "Don't be frightened," he commanded. "It's an earthquake! We learn about earthquakes up at school," and he opened his Bible to Matthew 24:7, and preached the signs of Christ's second coming.

"Soon Jesus is coming," he said, "and when He comes, no one shall be ignorant. He has sent His messengers, but we would not listen; He has sent us messages, but we would not read; and now God is talking in a voice we all must hear, that soon He is coming, and we must all get ready."

"Is that what it is? Is that what it is?" they said.

"But let us go and ask the priest." So they processioned their way to the Buddhist temple, only to find the priest white-faced and afraid like the others. "Ask me?" he said, "what do I know about earthquakes!"

"Well, let us go and ask the witch," they said. But the witch lay trembling with hysterics on her mat. "Oh, isn't it awful!" was all she could say. "Well, that's strange! The priest doesn't know, and the witch doesn't know, but Mg Thein, he knows," proudly called his father. "Don't you, Mg Thein? Here, stand up here and tell them all about the earthquake." And with the word of God in his hand, and the courage of God in his heart, Mg Thein preached the signs of Christ's second coming till after midnight. The crowd that once so angrily demanded the undoing of his baptism now readily assented with friendly grunts, and one by one, their earthquake fears all quieted, the crowd dispersed, and Mg Thein was left alone with his mother.

"Mg Thein, my son," she said, "mother doesn't like to see you leaving the house. To-morrow morning you will be going back to the school, so to-night mother is going to sleep in her brother's house. And in the morning you get up early and cook your rice; then as the sun is coming up on the horizon, go back to school. And mother won't have to watch you go away."

With this her voice choked, and Mg Thein went up into his house and, spreading his mat on the floor, lay down. But not to sleep,—his heart was too full. How true was this promise, "I will never leave thee, nor forsake thee"! How wonderfully had God wrought, to soften the hearts of his parents! Burying his face in his hands, he sobbed out his praise to God.